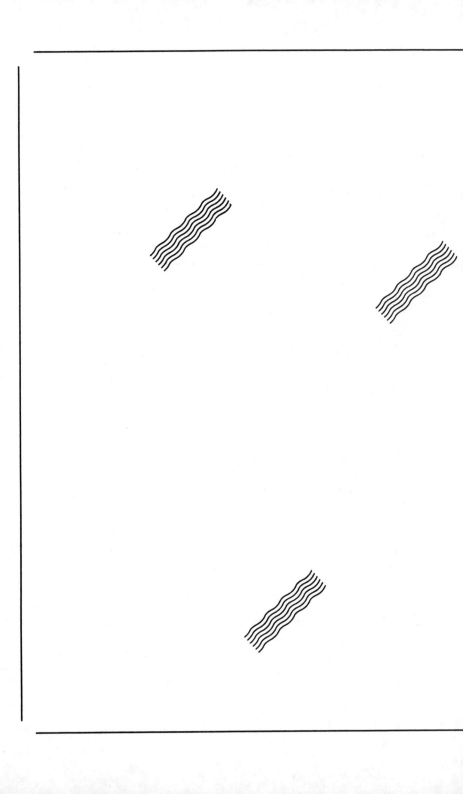

Deciphering the
SENSES

The Expanding World of
Human Perception

Robert Rivlin
Karen Gravelle

Simon and Schuster   New York

Library of Congress Cataloging in Publication Data
Rivlin, Robert.
    Deciphering the senses.
    Bibliography: p.
    Includes index.
    1. Senses and sensation.   2. Sense-organs.
3. Perception.   I. Gravelle, Karen.   II. Title.
AP431.R57   1984   152.1   84-1256
ISBN 0-671-49206-3

The authors are grateful to the following for permission to reproduce brief passages of text
from the copyrighted works named below:

The Bodley Head Ltd.: excerpts from Dante's *Purgatorio,* translated by John D. Sinclair, ©
1939, 1961.

University of California Press: excerpt from *The Teachings of Don Juan* by Carlos Castaneda.

Dover Publications: excerpt from *The Indians' Book* by Natalie Curtis, © 1968.

Fabulous Music Limited: excerpt from "See Me, Feel Me" by Peter Townshend. Copyright
© 1969 FABULOUS MUSIC LIMITED. All rights in the United States, its territories and
possessions, Canada, Mexico and The Philippines are controlled by Towser Tunes, Inc. All
Rights Reserved. International Copyright Secured. Reproduced by kind permission of Peter
Townshend, Fabulous Music Limited, and Towser Tunes, Inc.

Harcourt Brace Jovanovich: excerpt from *Modern Man in Search of a Soul* by C. G. Jung.

Harrap Ltd.: excerpt from *Witchcraft, Magic and Alchemy* by Grillot de Givry.

Penguin Books Ltd.: excerpts from *The Epic of Gilgamesh,* translated by N. K. Sandars
(Penguin Classics, Revised edition 1972), © 1960, 1964, 1972; excerpt from *The Senses* by
Otto Lowenstein, © 1966.

Princeton University Press: excerpts from *Shamanism: Archaic Techniques of Ecstasy,* translated
by Willard R. Trask, Bollinger Series 76, © 1964.

Grateful acknowledgment is made for permission to reproduce or adapt copyrighted illustra-
tions from the sources named:

"Multistability in Perception" by Fred Attneave. Copyright © 1971 by Scientific American,
Inc. All rights reserved.

© BEELDRECHT, Amsterdam/V.A.G.A., New York, Collection Haags Gemeentemusem
—The Hague, 1981.

Acknowledgments

The authors wish to thank the following, without whose help this work would never have come to pass: Robert Eckhardt for his undaunted confidence in the project, Peter Q. Herman, who prepared extensive material on the relationship between language and the sensory systems; Ric Gentry for his exclusive interview with cinematographer Vittorio Storaro; Michael Rivlin for his exclusive interview with Sam Boone (arranged by Eric and Christine Arnould); Dr. Bertram A. John for his invaluable suggestions and guidance throughout the entire research phase; Alice C. Wolf for her good sense of balance, which saw the manuscript through its most difficult periods; Eva J. Blinder for having given the manuscript its final polish; Toria Smith for her monumental typing effort; and Charles C. Lenz, Jr., for both time and resources.

The authors also thank Mary McAdam Keane for doing the drawings, Dana L. Kurtz for taking the photographs, and Janet Smith, Tim Wetmore, and Toria Smith for modeling.

Contents

Chapter One
The Seventeen Senses

Dolce color d'oriental zaffiro. . . .
The sweet hue of oriental sapphire which was gathering in
the serene face of the heavens from the clear zenith to the first
circle gladdened my eyes again as soon as I had passed out of
the dead air which had afflicted my eyes and breast.

Dante, PURGATORIO

The setting is an imaginary high school biology classroom some
twenty to twenty-five years ago. The teacher has just finished a two-
week unit on the chemistry of animal cells, and hopes that the
formula for respiration

$$\underset{C_6H_{12}O_6}{\text{carbohydrates}} + \underset{O_2}{\text{oxygen}} = \underset{CO_2}{\text{carbon dioxide}} + \underset{H_2O}{\text{water}} + \text{``ENERGY''}$$

(the basis of how organisms take food and convert it into energy) is
deeply engraved on every student's mind.

Now the focus of attention has turned to the next unit—the
senses. "There are five senses," begins the teacher. "Seeing, hearing,
feeling, tasting, and smelling. The last two are related, as you can
prove by holding your nose and seeing how little you actually taste
with your tongue. The tongue has specific areas on it that allow four
separate tastes: sweet, salty, bitter, and sour. All other 'tasting' is
done through the nose.

"The ear allows us to hear disturbances of the air which are vibrating from 20 to 20,000 times a second. We hear the difference in frequency as a difference in pitch, and a difference in the amplitude of the vibration as volume." The teacher demonstrates frequency and amplitude by taking a rope and moving it back and forth.

"Sounds strike the eardrum and are picked up and amplified by the three bones of the middle ear, which look like an anvil, a stirrup, and a hammer. The vibrations are passed along to the cochlea, or spiral canal, where they are translated into nerve impulses and carried back to the brain.

"The eyes allow us to see things by focusing light rays through the lens onto the sensitive part of the retina. Cells there pick up the images and send them back to the brain over the optic nerve. . . ."

At the time, of course, this account of the human sensory systems was perfectly adequate to satisfy all but the most inquisitive mind. But twenty short years later, it becomes obvious that those of us who were given this account were gypped, that these explanations fall far short of describing the real nature of the processes involved.

The deception probably wasn't intentional. Many of the discoveries that led to the more valid explanations were just being made. But unfortunately, the net result is the same—that it might have been better not to have learned any high school science at all, that the vast oversimplification of highly complex biological and chemical processes distorted them beyond usefulness. In the laboratory, we can burn carbohydrates to produce carbon dioxide and water; at no point during the complex process of cellular metabolism, however, does oxygen ever actually come into contact with carbohydrate molecules, nor does the cell give off carbon dioxide and water. Rather, in the Krebs cycle of cellular metabolism, the various molecules are first broken down, pass through several complex subprocesses, then are passed back out of the cell in constituent elements and reassembled only as the final stage before they are eliminated from the body.

The same oversimplification happened with the senses. Vision is not merely the action of the lens focusing light rays onto the retina;

rods and cones are involved, two completely distinct types of cells, derived from two distinct evolutionary functions, that account for contrast and color vision. Taste isn't just limited to sweet, salty, bitter, and sour. Hearing, olfaction, and touch are infinitely more complex than was suspected.

Thanks to a massive push in scientific research underway since the mid-1950s, much that was unknown about the human senses is finally becoming clear and accessible. Some of this research has been on the neurophysiological level and has led to significant new understanding of how the brain and nervous system work chemically, how neural transmitters carry coded messages between neurons, how nerve cells transmit impulses from the sense organs, how the sense organs transduce the various forms of mechanical, chemical, and electromagnetic energy in the environment into meaningful nerve impulses, how the brain's chemistry turns our attention to things worth noticing, and even how chemical processes combine to create consciousness itself. This is indeed the stuff that scientific dreams are made of—breakthrough research that actually explains the most basic aspects of human life.

The senses, according to the new definitions, perform the job of breaking down the continuum of reality into tiny, discrete pieces that can be analyzed by the sensory system's receptors, then reassembled in the brain into a coherent form again. On the one hand, the senses are highly precise, intricately programmed to provide an astonishingly detailed report on the part of nature to which they are sensitized. On the other hand, the senses sometimes seem like an astonishing Rube Goldberg-like collection of mechanical odds and ends that seem to have been thrown together almost capriciously. We hear because cells similar to shaving brushes push up against a membrane in response to wavelike motions in the inner ear. We taste because binder sites on the tongue attract molecules of foodstuffs like jigsaw puzzle pieces. We can tolerate enormous amounts of pain because a chemical secreted by the body prevents the sensation from being felt. It is almost impossible to imagine how evolution could have developed some of these mechanisms.

A perfect example of what this research has discovered is the true nature of the process of hearing—so astonishingly complex that it could as easily be a fantastic dream as scientific truth.

The basic function of the sense of hearing is to convert mechanical energy of fairly low frequency (the vibratory pattern in air, water, or solids created by striking one object against another, blowing air across the vocal cords, etc.) into the high-frequency electrical signals of the nervous system. The sense of hearing in man is closely allied to the ability of fish to "hear" the minute differences in water pressure that indicate movement or the ability of snakes to "hear" vibrations in the ground made by passing animals. The basic receptor mechanism in all these senses is a microscopic bundle of as many as 150 bristle-like spines arranged like a shaving brush protruding from the hair cell receptor. Arranged in different configurations in different body organs, the hair cell bundle is stimulated by mechanical pressure to emit the electrical impulses that signal the brain that a stimulus has been detected.

In humans, these same bristle structures are what give us a sense of balance and movement. We feel ourselves moving, for example, because of hair cells in two organs in the inner ear, one arranged horizontally and the other vertically. In each organ, the cells are embedded in a membrane separating two fluid-filled chambers. As the body (and thus the organ fluid) moves, the hair cells are bent. These cells are "directional" and react differently according to which side they are stimulated on (forward or backward, upward or downward). The same kind of mechanism is responsible for balance, with hair cells in the three semicircular canals detecting the differences in fluid motion in the horizontal, vertical, and diagonal orientations of the three canals.

Analyzing a sound involves the same kind of hair cells, arranged in an even more complex mechanism since two of the sound wave's properties must be specified by the transducer: the pitch of the sound, which depends on how rapidly the air is made to vibrate and therefore where on the vibrating basilar membrane the sound wave peaks occur; and the volume of the sound, which depends on how large the wave peaks are.

Perception of sound by the ear begins with the well-known pro-

cess by which the sound waves "beat" on the eardrum and cause it to vibrate. On the inner side of the eardrum are three small bones —said to resemble the hammer, anvil, and stirrup (the stapes) for which they are named—which pick up the movements of the eardrum and vibrate accordingly. The last of the bones in the series, the stirrup, has a flat end that rests on a membrane at one end of the cochlea, a spiral-shaped organ that is the actual center of the hearing mechanism.

The major new discovery about the hearing process has been about the exact mechanisms inside the cochlea. The hair cells responsible for hearing are located inside the cochlea in the organ of Corti, their bristles surrounded by the fluid in the cochlea and their bases embedded in the thick, rubbery basilar membrane. As a sound wave enters the cochlea by way of the stirrup and the membrane covering the cochlea's entrance, it causes wavelike activity in the cochlea's inner fluid—exactly like a wave generator used in a science lab. The wave motion of the fluid in turn causes the basilar membrane in the organ of Corti on which the hair cells are mounted to wave up and down. If the sound becomes louder, the wavelike motion of the fluid becomes stronger, and the membrane moves up and down with greater amplitude, oscillating in a wave pattern that mirrors the motion of the fluid.

The actual stimulation of the hair cells embedded in the membrane, however, depends on an even more impressive mechanism. Suspended just above the tips of the hair cells is a thin strip of cells called the tectorial membrane which forms a platelike extension over the hair cells. As the membrane carrying the hair cells moves up and down, it brushes the tips of the hair cells against this platelike covering, bending the hair cells down. The wavelike motion of the membrane results in corresponding wavelike patterns of the hair cells stimulated—and the larger the wave, the more hair cells are involved.

The final step in this process is the creation of an electrical spike inside the hair cell once it has been stimulated, accomplished by minute changes in the structure of the nerve cell wall that allow positively-charged chemicals to rush into the cell. The nervous sys-

tem carries this electrical spike back to the brain, where it is interpreted along with other nerve transmissions as representing a
particular pitch of a particular volume.

Work on hearing is just an example of the research going into
deciphering of some of the mysteries of the senses. But scientific
advance has been only part of the reason for this massive surge of
interest in the senses. Equally important has been a change in
consciousness itself.

It is as if Western society suddenly had both its literal and
figurative eyes opened in a collective consciousness-raising session
in the 1960s. Theories of perception and, indeed, perception itself,
ran head-first into mind-expanding, hallucination-producing psychedelic drugs, gurus from the East promising new heights of
awareness, and the awesome speculation about what an alien consciousness might perceive if it landed on earth.

Simultaneously, government-sponsored research, particularly for
the space program, directed toward robot vision, remote-sensing
systems, and measuring the capabilities of that perfect human spec-
imen, the astronaut, made the headlines and fired the imagination.

In addition, over the past few decades an entire generation has
grown up keenly aware of both the need for, and the excitement of,
scientific discovery. It is clear that the climate was just right for
what scientists—no longer old men working in musty laboratories,
but a new breed of hero—would shortly discover.

The significance of this change of attitude cannot be overempha-
sized, for it is here that the battle between science and magic, reason
and the mystery of life, rages most fiercely. For consciousness affects
not only what is acceptable as an explanation, but even what *can* be
known. For instance, some 500 years ago during the Medieval period and the Renaissance, philosophers knew of lenses and
their power to enlarge. But the eye itself was considered to distort
the godly, true, good image of the universe, as witnessed by count-
less optical illusions, and lenses were considered to distort the picture even more. Though they had the ability to create compound
lenses to make telescopes, the philosopher/scientists did not do so
for the view it would have given them of the planets would not have
been the view that God intended.

It was the same Medieval and Renaissance climate of thinking, in fact, that created the concept of the five senses. The basic idea was as old as Aristotle, with his notions of a "proper" plan for the universe. "By proper object I mean that which cannot be perceived by any other sense," he wrote, "e.g., sight is concerned with color, hearing with sound, and taste with flavor. Each sense has its proper sphere."

And, according to the Medieval philosopher Cornelius Agrippa, arguing Plato's philosophy, "Divinity is annexed to the mind, the mind to the intellect, the intellect to the intention, the intention to the imagination, the imagination to the senses, and the senses at last to things. For this is the bond and continuity of nature."

There was, in fact, a divine relationship between the senses and the world they sensed. And, like many things in God's divine plan for the universe, the senses were seen to occur in fives—a prime number with considerable symbolic significance. How convenient, then, to think of the body as having five senses, corresponding roughly to the sensory organs (eyes, ears, nose, tongue, and skin). That the skin could feel both temperature and touch, to say nothing of pain, was somehow conveniently overlooked in order to align the essential unity of the human body with a metaphysical plan of the universe; to say we had eight or eighteen senses simply wouldn't do.

Nor was there a lack of evidence suggesting that there might be other sensory systems. As early as the 1700s, for example, there were reports of cases of eidetic imagery, the ability to see an image after it has been removed from the visual field. Even in the 1930s when the eidetic ability was being fully explored, perception was still being taught as "the five senses."

Evidence abounded, too, that other species were able to perceive magnetic fields, or infrared radiation, or electrical energy, and that humans might have vestiges of some of these sensory systems. Even as researcher after researcher pointed to the validity of psychic abilities of various types, they continued to be thought of as *extra*-sensory perceptions, outside the scope of "normal" sensory experiences. Society was not yet ready for, nor did it need, anything more than five.

One of the clearest instances of how lack of consciousness itself prevented a more accurate picture of the senses is the example of the trigeminal system, the specialized network of nerves that carries information about touch and temperature sensations in the face and head. And consider oral gratification. In the classic description of the senses, it is taste and odor that account for most of our interest in food. But although this simple explanation is true, research is proving once again that there is a lot more to oral gratification than just taste and smell. How, for instance, can taste or smell account for the pleasure we get from all the other oral activities in which we constantly engage—from smoking to nail-biting to mustache-licking to teeth-picking? But how else can oral gratification be accounted for in a model of the sensory system that has only five receptor systems?

The answer, of course, is that it cannot. In oral stimulation, taste and smell are not really responsible at all. Instead, it is the stimulation of another, completely separate sensory system associated with the trigeminal nerves that comes into play in oral gratification. The actual texture of food in the mouth may be at least as important as its chemical nature in determining how it is perceived.

Somewhere along the way, of course, consciousness *did* change. Partially because of the seminal scientific research, partly because of changes in consciousness, the "truth" about the senses has come to light. Scientific investigators, freed of the restraint of conforming to an outmoded world view, can now describe a number of major sensory systems in addition to the five that had been so firmly rooted in thought since the Renaissance. These new systems include the vomeronasal system, capable of detecting pheromones (chemical signals given off to indicate intraspecific messages such as sexual receptivity, fear, identification); nociception (a separate sensory system for pain, distinct from touch and temperature sensing); parallel but separate sensory systems for experiencing thermal and tactile sensations; parallel but separate systems for detecting the visual contour/contrast/form of an object and its color; the existence of a functional pineal gland in humans, able to respond to light and synchronize internal body rhythms to the rhythms of the sun; and so forth.

It has even become apparent that some of the supposedly mystical abilities of extra-sensory perception (ESP)—sensitivity to magnetic fields, ability to detect auras, and so forth—could also be explained as the result of still undiscovered sensory systems—either degenerated vestiges of senses found in other animals or totally human sensory systems that are still evolving into a more sophisticated form. Five was obviously just not enough to account for the huge range of sensory possibilities of which the human species is capable; seventeen senses is probably a more accurate count.

At the same time that these previously hidden sensory systems were being brought to light, there was also a tremendous surge in discoveries about what was possible with the already known systems such as smell, touch, and taste. What on the surface level had been explained with such simplicity ("the taste buds, each sensitive to a different kind of substance . . .") was suddenly discovered to be infinitely more detailed, and infinitely richer. Taste, for example, turned out to be among the most complex of the sensory systems.

The basic controversy in taste theory had been evident almost as long as it had been realized that taste is sensitive to only four quite specific sensations: sweet, sour, salty, and bitter. (Smell, of course, can perceive far more complex chemical molecules.) At least as far back as the 1800s, however, scientists had been arguing about whether these four types of sensation are actually separate taste sensations, or whether they are merely points along a continuous spectrum (as, for example, the colors red, orange, yellow, and green are points in the continuous spectrum of visible light).

If the taste receptors are indeed separate, then a mixture of sweet and sour should produce both sweet and sour tastes—as if there were two separate sensory systems at work. If the four types of sensations are merely points along the same continuum, taste mixtures should produce sensations in which the flavors are blended and in which a taste different from either of the two ingredients is perceived (as is the case with color). Apparently no empirical test can be devised that conclusively proves that we do or do not perceive tastes separately.

As with so much of modern thinking on the senses, this debate comes down to a dispute over the sensory receptors themselves, in this case the taste buds. The first theories on the physiology of taste evolved at a time when the great discoveries of nineteenth-century physiology were just getting underway. For the first time, scientists began to understand the human body not as a simple, unanalyzable unit but as a series of discrete parts and systems that could each be described separately. Taste was isolated from smell, and the individual taste sensations were further analyzed into discrete systems. Areas on the tongue were labeled as being more sensitive to one or another of the four tastes, and separate nerve bundles were thought to carry information about each of the four back to the brain.

This description, of course, corresponded with the view that there are four separate taste functions rather than a continuum of sensation. It was a mechanistic explanation produced by the science of the age of factory assembly lines—the machine age in which the whole could be broken down into discrete parts and analyzed.

As knowledge of physiology progressed, however, the pendulum swung. In the 1940s it was discovered that each of the nerve fibers leading back to the brain carry information about at least two types of taste stimuli and are not restricted to a single kind of information as the "four separate taste sensations" theory would suggest.

How does the brain distinguish sweet from sour if the same nerve fiber carries both kinds of information? It does so by means of an incredible Morse code-like scheme in which two sets of nerve impulses combine to form each type of sensation; since one type of nerve will respond to sweet and sour, for instance, and another to sweet and salty, when signals are received from both nerves the "sweet" message is received while "salty" and "sour" are rejected.

This "pattern theory," which has its exact parallels in every aspect of sensory research, including the latest thinking on pain, evolved at a time when the popular science was quantum physics, a science whose view of the world was that it was no longer sufficient simply to have an understanding of the discrete parts to understand the whole; a knowledge of the larger, sometimes hidden forces at work was also essential.

The new discoveries on taste, however, have seen the pendulum shift again—perhaps mirroring another shift in general scientific research back to the particles and parts of matter (there are now even gravitons, which are said to be elementary particles of gravity that glue the universe together). For although the various taste nerve fibers *are* sensitive to different types of sensations, they are *most* sensitive to only one kind. Thus, each taste-sensitive nerve leading back to the brain actually can be classified as to which of the four types of sensation it carries information about.

Thus, for now, the explanation appears to be that there are four distinct types of taste sensations, each with its own set of nerves that report best about what is perceived as a discrete part of the environment.

As for some of the specific phenomena of taste, one of the most important questions being worked on, by Linda Bartoshuk of Yale University's John B. Pierce Laboratories, is, simply, why certain foods taste good to some people but are not appealing to others. Plainly, some of this difference in taste is due to upbringing and culture, so that it has only been relatively recently, for instance, that Japanese-style raw fish has been palatable to Americans, although raw clams and oysters have always been acceptable. It is the thought of eating "raw fish" that apparently is distasteful, whereas "oysters on the half-shell" (as opposed to "raw oysters") are fine.

Some tastes, however, are simply different for different people—a result of differences in the tasting mechanism itself. Heredity may have provided you with a neurological sensitivity to a substance found in artichokes (and to a lesser extent in asparagus) that produces a sweet sensation when water is drunk after eating them. Heredity is also responsible for allowing only two-thirds of us to sense the bitter taste of phenylthiocarbamide (PTC), a taste sense apparently linked to finding bitter such substances as caffeine and saccharin. A certain small percentage of people have a supersensitivity for these bitter-tasting substances, accounting for the unpleasant effect diet soft drinks can have on some people.

That these variations are possible is also demonstrated by individual tastes for salt. This is regulated by the amount of salt in each person's saliva—a level which fluctuates according to individual body chemistry, amount of exercise, and so forth. The more sodium that is present, the more accustomed we become to it, and therefore the more sodium we require in foods to give them a salty taste. Individual salt preferences are therefore based on highly personal factors. And children who do not "develop a taste for salt" or do not need to sprinkle it on food until later in life may simply have such low levels in their saliva that they can taste the naturally-occurring sodium in foods.

This mechanism for adjusting salt levels is not the same for bitterness and the other tastes, however. If you were to eat a large quantity of salt, after a certain point your salt-tasting ability would become overloaded and no more sensations would get through. This is true no matter whether plain table salt (sodium chloride) or other salts such as monosodium glutamate are used. If, on the other hand, taste is saturated with one form of bitterness—quinine, for instance —although quinine itself can no longer be sensed, other bitter tastes such as potassium continue to be experienced. It may be because so many poisonous substances in nature are bitter-tasting (cyanide, arsenic) that adaptive evolution has made us more able to discriminate in the range of bitter tastes.

The most significant set of findings to date, however, may be the discovery of the chemical processes by which tasting actually takes place. In the latest model, salt and sour, and bitter and sweet are sensed by quite different processes.

Common salt, for instance, is made up of a sodium molecule and a chloride molecule, forming sodium chloride. But saltiness results when NaCl is broken down into its constituent parts when dissolved in water (saliva); it is sodium that activates the salt-sensitive taste buds. Further, certain chemicals can inhibit taste sensations, so that monosodium glutamate (MSG), which contains far more sodium than table salt, actually tastes less salty because the glutamate in-hibits the sodium-sensing reaction.

With sourness, much the same process is involved. Here it is the sour-tasting acid substance—ascorbic acid (Vitamin C), acetic acid (vinegar), citric acid, and so forth—that is broken down into its elemental group (hydrogen, for example, in hydrochloric acid), and its chloride group. It is actually the effect of the hydrogen that causes the sour taste.

Sweet and bitter tastes, on the other hand, are stimulated directly by molecules of various food substances and do not need to be broken down to be tasted. Just as there are different sensitivities for the bitter substances, so there seem to be at least two different kinds of receptors and nerve pathways for different types of sugars.

The extent to which science can now explain the process of tasting is demonstrated by the common "toothpaste/orange juice effect," in which orange juice can taste quite unpleasant in the morning just after brushing one's teeth. One of the functions of detergents is to break down the structure of fat so it can be washed away. Many toothpastes contain detergents, which help dissolve food particles and the like. Unfortunately, the composition of the taste bud membrane is a fat-based phospholipid, and the toothpaste actually temporarily breaks down the structure of the membrane, interfering with the taste of sugar in the juice. The unpleasantness is further magnified by other chemicals in the toothpaste which make the orange's ascorbic and citric acid taste bitter and sour.

We have spent so much time on taste because it is typical of a sensory system that is often taken for granted, but which modern research is revealing as a complex set of interrelationships between the body and the environment which can lead to profound new understandings of both. But these observations about the sense(s) of taste (it's possible to make a case for considering sweet, salty, bitter, and sour each as separate sensory systems) are just the minutiae of far larger questions—namely, what is the relation between reality and our perception of it, and what is the relation between one sensory system and another?

As for the former, an organism's sensory systems are now seen to provide only a more-or-less detailed interior model of the portion of "reality" that enables that organism to exist within it. Not a view of the ultimate reality itself (if there is such a thing), but a highly filtered, highly selective, often distorted view which is geared to one goal only: species survival. It takes only the simplest example —that humans have no direct sensitivity to infrared radiation, but some snakes do—to show just how limited the world-view of each species really is.

This understanding leads us closer than ever before to an understanding of how the senses relate to one another. In the modern view, the senses are simply a set of measuring instruments tuned to different aspects of the natural world. They are, in fact, electronic transducers which transform different types of energy found in the physical universe—mechanical pressure, chemical bonding, thermal gradation, electromagnetic radiation of various sorts, etc.— into electrical impulses that can be interpreted by the brain.

The validity of this understanding of the sensory systems is made quite clear by some of the spectacular recent achievements in the fields of artificial intelligence and robot sensing. The general philosophical considerations of robotics do not concern us here, for they are primarily concerned with the inner functions of the logical (and even emotional) thought processes. But how does an artificial intelligence perceive its environment? Through robot eyes and robot ears and artificial sensory systems that are the rival of our own.

Robot vision has been available for a number of years, an outgrowth of basic television technology. The visual field is focused by a lens onto a small imaging device, where it is scanned rapidly by an electron beam. Differences between light and dark are encoded as differences in a basic flow of electricity in the beam, setting up a modulated current that represents the contrast in the visual field. Color imaging is achieved by splitting the light rays in their red, green, and blue components through a prism, then directing the refracted light to three separate tubes that analyze the color components separately.

The string of modulated electronic data is then converted into digital information by reading the value of the analog signal at a predetermined number of times a second (the "clock" rate); if the analog signal ranges on an arbitrary scale from 0 to 100, the digitally-converted signal might use eight-bit digital "words" to represent each step on the scale (00000000, 00000001, 00000011, 00000111, and so forth). The digital information representing the image is then fed into a computer memory, and compared with data representing objects that the programmer wants the robot to recognize. When the data matches, the object is "recognized" and the robot takes appropriate action.

As might be expected, problems arise when objects overlap, since the data in the essentially two-dimensional vision system does not know where the outline of one object begins and where another one ends. More sophisticated systems are therefore being built that recognize not only the outline shapes but individual, "local" details of an object such as surface markings and textures. Added to the programs that recognize outlines, the programs that recognize markings make identification that much easier. At the same time, yet other programs take the data that has entered through the television camera eye and shrink, enlarge, and rotate it in order to see if it will then fit the data in its memory. In one system with military applications, the basic outline shapes for several different types of aircraft are entered into the memory. When the vision system "notices" movement in the sky, it turns its camera toward that sector and feeds the data into the vision system—an exact parallel to the human process whereby attention is directed toward a moving object in the environment. The computer then scales and positions the object represented by the data until it corresponds to the basic outline shape, at which point it positively identifies the aircraft.

The significance of this research in robot sensing is not only the development of better machines, however. It is also providing a key to the understanding of the human process of perception. For if one took all that is known or is likely to be known about human taste, for example, it still would be only a series of chemical reactions and their conversion into nerve impulses; without the interpretive action of the brain, no perception—only raw sensing—would take place. It is in the brain itself that science's major discoveries about the senses are being made.

The parallel in robotics is the research that is allowing robots to break out of the typically two-dimensional world into the world of three-dimensional spatial relationships. Some systems project laser light onto objects, measuring the time it takes for the energy to return from different parts of the object—a system not unlike that used by bats and dolphins to echolocate. Another system called ACRONYM, developed at Stanford University, uses a pattern of light projection in which the light reflected by the object is distorted in a characteristic pattern that allows the vision system to distinguish between curved and angular surfaces. The most sophisticated system, however, uses two cameras positioned side-by-side to provide a stereoscopic, three-dimensional image based on the minute differences in angle between the two images—virtually identical to the way humans get most of their depth cues.

The relevance of all this to human perception is that the brain's cognitive functions also appear to be set up in computer-like modeling programs that organize incoming sensory data into meaningful patterns. The brain doesn't contain templates that match external reality one-to-one; according to Gestalt psychologists, however, apparently innate organizing processes insure that foreground and background are distinguished from one another, that the curved sides of a ball are perceived to form the single shape of a sphere, and so forth.

The parallel between robot and human perception is not limited to vision alone. Touch, too, has its parallels in a "robot finger" developed by William Hillis and John Hollerbach at MIT that uses a printed circuit board with tiny microswitches in place of nerve endings. When the "finger" touches an object, certain of the switches are closed while others remain open—allowing the microprocessor "brain" to interpret the pattern of open and closed switches as the details of a solid object.

The analogy between robot senses and human senses, artificial intelligence and human intelligence is, of course, not all that surprising considering that man has created the robot in his own image. But in a certain sense, the collective power of literally millions of man-hours of development and programming may have created what no one individual or small group of individuals could create on their own. Indeed, robots and computers may actually represent the collective inner workings of the human nervous system projected into the external form of embodied digital technology.

This makes the robot worthy of even closer study—for what it reveals of the human nervous system that self-analysis might not pick up.

In this light, the bioelectronic nature of human sensory systems and the brain are easily understood—even in a system as complex as vision. In the eye, electromagnetic radiation of many different frequencies (including X-rays, cosmic rays, visible light, infrared radiation, etc.) is focused on the retina by the lens. The retina's cells are each responsive to a certain radiation frequency which, when summed together, comprises what we see as "visible light."

As the light falls on a particular cell—one responsive to blue light, for example—the cell's blue-sensitive molecular pigments absorb photons of light in the blue region of the spectrum. The photon energy causes a biochemical change in which the pigment momentarily transmutes to a slightly different substance. Then, microseconds later as the pigment returns to its normal state, the photon energy becomes a miniature bioelectrical spike in the retina cell. Through a process that will be revealed in more detail in the following chapters, the electrical impulse is then conducted along the nervous system to the brain where the message is combined with those from other receptors to signal the perception of blue light. Added together with other impulses from other nerves, and after considerable processing, an actual image of the world outside is formed inside the brain.

Each of the senses works in a similar way, converting a particular type of chemical, mechanical, or electromagnetic energy into electrical impulses that are passed along to the brain for interpretation. And the brain itself interprets the data as if it were the central processing unit in a computer system whose terminals and various input/output devices were the sensory systems.

For some, of course, this view is far too mechanistic—a rational explanation for processes that are essentially mysterious and the workings of a larger, perhaps divine force. And indeed, an explanation of human sensory systems that is so rooted in the current wave of popular science—the digital, electronics era in which the all-pervasive computer has taken so strong a foothold—may be suspect.

In another culture in another time, one in which no electronics had been discovered, another explanation might suffice perfectly adequately. Ancient Chinese philosophers who knew nothing of modern science discovered acupuncture and described the healing "fluids" it released throughout the body when the acupuncture needles were inserted. We today know these fluids as endorphins, or endogenous opiates—substances produced by the body in response to stimulation by acupuncture needles that literally block the brain from feeling a pain. But is this explanation any more or less valid than the healing fluid theory of many centuries ago? It simply suits the frame of our current thinking more adequately.

But given that biochemical and bioelectrical processes do satisfy certain basic levels of explanation about how the body works, let us see just how far the model can be extended. Indeed, it is valid all the way to the top—the very mechanism within the brain itself that apparently accounts for perception. The human body is still a sacred, mysterious organism, and the process by which *Cogito ergo sum* (I think therefore I am) takes place is still the ultimate unanswered question of creation. But modern science has at least identified some of the mechanisms if not the actual process by which thought takes place, and along with it the process by which we perceive the world. If one is looking for the divine plan of the human sensory systems, this is as close as science in the 1980s can come.

The plan, quite simply, is that the brain's cerebral cortex, the part that thinks as well as processes sensory data, is organized according to a systematic topographical plan that corresponds to the arrangement of cells within the sensory systems and thence to the world they perceive. Each of the brain's maps devoted to a particular sense is made up of nerve endings that correspond geographically to the part of the body where the nerve impulses originate. Thus, in the part of the cortex that handles pressure and touch information from the skin and internal body structures such as muscles and joints, there are individual areas reserved for each body part. Each hand, for example, has its own area set aside, and the area for the right hand lies somewhere close to the area for the right arm. And within the part assigned to the right hand, each finger also has its own area, geographically adjacent to the other fingers.

The subdivisions go even further. Within the area reserved for the fingers, there are actually two alternating strips of nerve layers that respond to different types of sensations—one the more specific sensation associated with touch, the other a "deeper" kind of feeling that allows us to be conscious that the hand is there if we need it. These two sets of maps are each complete unto themselves, but exist side by side in alternating layers of nerve cells.

The same principle applies in the visual cortex where information from the left and right eye converge. Alternating bands process information from left and right eye, so that the data from each is almost completely segregated, until the very final stage when another processing center compares left- and right-eye vision and produces a comparison that enables depth perception of the environment. But within the visual cortex, information received from the right visual field of the right eye is kept very close to information received from the right visual field of the left eye; the visual cortex actually contains a map of the retinas arranged so that top and bottom, left and right of the visual field comes out just that way in the brain. In other words, although one cannot get a direct representation of the world by simply reading out the information from cells in the visual cortex, the patterns of nerve firings there do definitely contain a specific reference to the configuration of the natural world; light from top and bottom, left and right of an object, because it falls on appropriate cells in the retina, is translated into the correct spatial orientation in the cortex.

The most superficial look at a modern computer reveals a structure so similar to this organization of the brain that one wonders if computer designers had precognitive experiences with biological discoveries that were to come years later. The sensory systems are the brain's input devices, like terminals connected to the central processing unit (CPU). Terminals/sensory systems connect with specific parts of the central brain/CPU operating system, allowing them to function individually within the system, but networking them together so that input information can be shared. The programs are all similar, being based on the same digital processing logic; but each performs a specific task which can be kept separated from the others. In the final data-processing stage, however, programs are combined and the output created as a single unified data base.

Is this explanation of the senses, perception, and consciousness a cold, "inhuman" view that no humanist could coexist with (as some have suggested concerning all things that have to do with computers)? We began this overview of the latest trends in scientific thinking on the senses with the observation that Renaissance philosophers, in their zeal to organize nature and man into neat, discrete, easily labeled categories, had created the false idea of "the five senses" that had persisted into recent times. But just as modern scientific thinking has exploded the myth of the five senses, it is now on the verge of creating a new universal truth about the senses, every bit as satisfying as the concept it so vehemently denied. Now there are seventeen senses, now they are unified by principles of electronic transduction, now the brain operates according to the laws of electrical induction rather than the laws of God. But the result is the same.

And ultimately it is the ancient philosophy of the Middle Ages that may provide the answer—a universal truth in human consciousness that seems almost mystical but is proven time and again. Wholeness, radiance, and harmony, said the philosophers, are the three processes of all nature. In the beginning, the object is seen in its wholeness—like the Renaissance view of the five senses as part of the basic operating principle of the natural world whose laws all living things obeyed. The next step is radiance—the object is seen in its various pieces and components, analyzed separately and individually, as has been the case with modern science's approach to sensory systems. But finally the object is seen in harmony—the separate pieces woven together into a fabric in which each has a place, in which each can be appreciated as a separate system, but which obey a set of laws common to all the elements within it.

Chapter Two
Pain

Another province of the mechanical sense still full of unsolved problems is pain. The baffling nature of pain becomes strikingly clear when one considers the reports of patients who have lost a limb by amputation, but can still feel and localize so-called phantom pain in a finger or toe of the long-lost limb. It is clear that free nerve endings must be chiefly involved in the reception of painful stimuli, because pain is registered by parts of the body exclusively supplied by them. On the other hand, it is well known that in the last resort all sensory structures can evoke painful sensations on overstimulation.

Otto Lowenstein, THE SENSES

Pain. It is an almost universal phenomenon. Cross-cultural, historical, projectible into the future of the species. Some ten to twenty million Americans alone live with it on a daily basis—chronic headaches, back pain, migraine attacks, arthritis. Almost half the American adult population reaches for temporary relief from acute pain each year—toothaches, ulcers, headaches, pulled muscles, the thousand natural shocks that flesh is heir to. Few will die without at least one profound sensory experience of pain.

But what exactly is pain? This is a question that has perplexed researchers for centuries. It is, of course, a definitely physical sensation, a sensory experience like seeing and hearing. But just as there are optical illusions, so are there the many illusions of pain. And it becomes clear that perception of pain is as much a cognitive experience as it is a physical one. For while there are biochemical and physiological processes at work, "feeling pain" most definitely involves emotional feelings as well as physical ones. Indeed, the psychological part of the experience can be isolated from the physical part and studied separately.

Just how large a role these mental processes play can be gauged by how different women respond to menstrual cramps. For many women with traditional values, the menstrual cycle is part of their identity as women, and the pain of menstrual cramps is a reaffirmation of that identity. For women attempting to redefine their roles, on the other hand, cramps are no longer important to their self-image, and the perception of the pain is often considerably reduced.

Then there is the well-known phenomenon of phantom-limb pain in which victims of amputation or accidental loss of limb report still feeling pain in the missing part with as much intensity as if it were real and still needed attention.

Or consider the amazing feats offered up as "magic" in so many cultures in which fakirs or witches or religious zealots walk on fiery coals or lie on beds of crushed glass or pierce their skin with skewers, apparently convinced psychologically that they feel no pain even though the skin is broken and pain should be felt. And there are the incredible stories of those who experience extreme trauma such as having a limb severed and feel nothing until some time after the event has occurred.

These experiences of not feeling discomfort are part of another universal aspect of pain—the truly epic search for a way to cure or prevent it. In order to put a single medicine on the market, a major pharmaceutical company will spend millions of dollars in the various testing procedures demanded by the Food and Drug Administration. Painkillers are big business. Americans spend one billion-plus dollars annually on over-the-counter products such as aspirin and Tylenol to treat headaches and pain arising from skin or muscular/skeletal damage. Excedrin alone claims that sixty thousand people an hour, one million a day use its product. And pharmacies do a multimillion-dollar business in the opioids (forms of morphine and codeine) and substances such as steroids that work in conjunction with actual painkillers in cases of muscular/skeletal damage.

On the most basic level, of course, there is a general consensus, backed up by good common sense, that pain is an indication that something is wrong, that tissue damage has occurred or is about to occur. There are exceptions—pain that is purely psychosomatic in nature and has no physical manifestation, for example. The latest theory on headaches, too, suggests that they are caused by a disruption in the body's own pain-sensing mechanism rather than muscular contraction or blood vessel swelling. And, in the instance of "referred pain," a person will feel intense pain in a part of the body that is not directly affected—searing pain in the back and shoulders caused by heart problems, for instance. The latest theory on this condition is that messages from both parts of the body somehow get "cross-wired" in the spinal cord so that the brain doesn't know where the real pain message is coming from.

But pain is generally an alarm bell that indicates not only that there is a problem, but also where it lies. The problem may be outside the body—a fire, for instance, in which case pain receptors in the skin are stimulated directly by conditions in the environment. Or the source of the problem may be within the body itself, a disease causing damage to organs or muscles whose deterioration also stimulates pain receptors. Or pain can result from the swelling of blood vessels which in turn exert pressure on pain receptors.

Pain is a largely beneficial experience. It demands that we do something to alleviate the problem that causes it—take the finger out of the flame, rub a banged elbow, see a doctor, and so on. Again there are exceptions, such as chronic pain in which the original cause of the damage is no longer a concern but the pain persists anyway. But a sense of acute pain, as disturbing as it is, is the body's first means of protecting itself against even further damage.

Beyond this most simple level of understanding, however, fundamental questions about pain remained unanswered throughout centuries of science. Looking back through the annals of medical history, it is as if pain were so commonplace that it barely merited mentioning. At most, pharmacists and men of medicine invented ways of soothing it with salves and medicines that had little to do with its actual causes.

Certainly it was not included in early science's scheme of the five senses. Explanations of pain, therefore, portrayed it as overstimulation of the same nerves that carried information about other sensations—in other words, not really a separate sensory system at all. The same nerve endings that produced a sensation of warmth were thought, if enough of them were given enough stimulation, to produce a sensation of burning and pain. The nerve endings that responded to touch would produce pain if the skin were cut, and a slightly different sensation if a large number were stimulated simultaneously as with a slap.

The theory, of course, was wrong. But it is worth observing again, as we did earlier when considering the evolution of thinking on the sense of taste, that scientific thought and research, as with any human endeavor, can only reflect the cultural and perceptual paradigms of the day, and ask the questions that the society is capable of posing. Surely the observation that the world worked according to the will and pleasures of the god Zeus was as satisfying to the ancient Greeks as our own theories are to us, and were every bit as "accurate"; it is merely that our more sophisticated culture demands more sophisticated explanations, fed in turn by scientific advances that change our cultural perceptions.

The problem with the theory that burning was just an overabundance of warmth was that it simply could not explain the burning feeling produced by too much cold. And what could account for pain inside the body that was completely unrelated to other tactile sensations? Just as science would come to discover the atom with its discrete, tangible particles, so the solution to these questions about pain was the discovery that the body had a set of pain receptors connected to a sensory system separate from that which carried information about touch and temperature.

Aided by improvements in the microscope, scientists discovered what were interpreted as four separate types of nerve receptors in the skin, corresponding to the four skin-based senses (a number reminiscent of the four kinds of taste sensations described earlier).

Touch had its own receptors—corpuscle-like nerve endings. Heat sensors were cylindrically shaped. For cold sensing there were Krauss "end bulbs." And, for pain, unconnected with the other tactile and thermal sensors, undifferentiated free nerve endings were the receptor mechanism. Pain, like the skin's several other tactile and thermal systems, was therefore defined as separate.

Not only did research uncover four separate and distinct receptors, but also separate nerve pathways to carry the information back to the spinal cord and brain. Neurons carrying information about pain were shown to first pass through clusters of nerve cells in the spine (ganglia) where they made contact with nerves controlling the muscular system; in this way urgent information ("take finger out of fire") could be acted on immediately although seconds might elapse before the pain message could get to the brain and the sensation "pain" be registered and verbalized.

This line of thinking about pain perception—that it is based on specific nerve endings and specific nerve pathways—was definitely on the right track. As with many oversimplifications that attempt to establish precise mechanical corollaries for bodily processes, however, it represented more the desire to neatly explain things than it did good science or even good sense. Besides, society no longer felt such a pressing need for the concrete. Science was becoming almost mystical in its approach, as witnessed by the quantum theory, and looking for a more coherent, holistic cosmos than particle and sensory specificity theory would allow.

The next wave of pain research therefore uncovered a brand-new explanation of the pain-sensing process. One of the main problems with specificity theory is that there are obviously more than the four kinds of tactile and thermal stimulations corresponding to the four types of skin receptors that the researchers had originally found. Besides warmth, touch, pain and cold, there are itch, tickle, different types of pain (burning/searing, stabbing/sharp, throbbing/aching, etc.), as well as a sensitivity to vibration. Armed with this logic, the new wave of pain research did indeed discover that there are many more than four types of skin receptors. Actually, there is a whole continuum of receptor types of which the four main types are merely the most exaggerated forms. It was clear, then, that the various skin-based senses could not act independently, as specificity theory had suggested, if they did not have separate receptors dedicated to them.

Another problem with the specificity theory was its inability to explain sensitivity in the eye. The cornea (the outer part of the eyeball) contains free nerve endings almost exclusively, the receptors thought to account for pain sensitivity. How, then, was the cornea also able to sense touch and heat?

Further, it was discovered, once scientists began looking for the evidence, that *all* nerve receptors are sensitive to at least some types of pressure—even those supposedly reserved for hot and cold sensing. And all receptors are somewhat sensitive to changes in temperature (true of any biochemical system), even those that had been thought reserved especially for mechanical stimulation such as touch. Further, stripped of the sheaths that define their different shapes, nerves still transmit impulses.

The new theory that was evolved suggested that all neural receptors were sensitive to a broad range of stimuli. And, rather than having "dedicated nerves" each devoted to a particular sensation, the body's tactile and thermal pathways all shared the same nerves, with different sensations distinguished by a codelike patterning of neuro-electrical energy.

By measuring the response pattern of large nerve cells in the spinal cord, pain was shown to result in highly irregular bursts of nerve activity with irregular spacing between the bursts. Itching, on the other hand, produced a rapid but highly regular pattern. Heating was shown to produce a steady increase in neural activity as the heating increased, while light pressure produced a burst of nerve activity when the stimulus was first applied; harder pressure simply increased the length of time the initial burst lasted rather than increasing the frequency of nerve firings.

These findings mirror the tremendous changes society had undergone in its progress from the mechanical to the electronic age, and the discoveries about the activity of nerve cells were seen to closely correspond to electrical circuits. In the same way that the eye transforms the radiant energy of light into the bioelectrical energy of the nervous system, so the nerve cells in the skin were also recognized to be transducers, converting physical energy (a touch or a burn, for example) into electrical energy. Once in electrical form, the nerve impulse is carried to the spinal cord and brain over nerve fibers (neurons) that resemble electrical wires. The neuron cell in its resting state is a "leaky condenser" with a negative charge of around -70 millivolts (about one tenth the power of a flashlight battery). Achieved by biological "pumps" pushing positively-charged sodium out of the cell, the electrical gradient is maintained by the nerve cell's two-molecule-thick membrane that normally keeps the sodium out and negatively-charged substances in.

When the nerve's threshold level is reached, however—when there is a stimulus strong enough to make it react—there is a rapid change resulting in a depolarization in the cell's membrane around the area of stimulation: sodium is allowed to rush into the nerve cell through small channels in the membrane, instantly changing its polarity from negative to positive. The positive charge in the affected part of the cell in turn causes the membrane in the next part of the cell to allow sodium in, while the part affected first quickly returns to normal. Thus, a spike of positively-charged electrical energy is passed along the length of the nerve.

This process of discovery, which did not really conclude until the early 1960s, also showed how more "sophisticated" nerves, with insulating sheaths, work even faster. At breaks in the sheath, a portion of the electrical spike can leave the nerve and move out into the surrounding body fluid, reentering the nerve again at the next break in the sheath and preparing the membrane there for the rest of the electrical pulse.

At the junctions between nerve cells, the research showed both electrical and chemical processes at work to get the electrical spike across the gap (synapse) between the nerve cells. As the Morse code-like message of electrical spikes reaches the end of the nerve, it is transformed into a more graded electrical impulse. This electrical charge, in turn, causes the release of neural transmitters, biochemical substances that migrate across the gap and are received by neural

receivers on the other side. At the receiver sites, the neural transmitters cause a depolarization triggering the codelike electrical signals, and the nerve impulse continues along its way.

A major breakthrough in pain research itself was the discovery
that the major neural transmitters of pain are serotonin and probably
dopamine and norepinephrine. Three other substances, histamine,
prostaglandin, and bradykinin, present in the nerves and synapses
closer to the skin receptor sites also act as mediators in conveying
information about pain.

Other substances in the synapse cause it to act like a capacitor or
transistor (devices in electronic circuits that accumulate electrical
charges or impede their flow). Thus, the synapse can be "loaded"
with drugs to alter or block nerve transmissions passing through it.
Certain drugs have been shown to interfere with the production of
the neural transmitters themselves, or to occupy the receptor sites
so that the transmitter cannot be received. Abnormal levels of catecholamines, for example, can account for mood disturbances, with
depression resulting from too little of the transmitter and mania
from too much. Lithium, a drug used to treat manic-depressives,
blocks the release of one of these catecholamines called norepinephrine.

Cocaine creates part of its effect because of its action at the
synapse. Normally, once a neural transmitter has been released by
one nerve and received by another, the excess left over in the synapse
is either broken down or reabsorbed by the nerve cell that released
it. Cocaine, together with drugs such as amphetamines and Elavil,
interferes with this mechanism. The left-over transmitter continues
to stimulate the receiver nerves, particularly in the central nervous
system where messages about heart rate, blood pressure, and so
forth are being carried. LSD and other hallucinogens also operate at
the junction between nerves, affecting the encoding and decoding
process so that neural messages are altered.

One of the most significant discoveries as far as pain is concerned
is the mechanism that accounts for lateral inhibition. In the eye,
ear, and skin, sensory receptors not only make connections with
nerves leading eventually to the brain, but they also make lateral
synapses with adjacent receptors. These lateral connections inhibit

rather than activate the neighboring cell. Thus, cells adjacent to each other can mutually reduce the impulses each can send toward the brain.

This interaction is what happens when looking at an image with highly contrasting forms, such as a black circle on a white background, for example. The area just inside the black circle appears to be far more intensely black while the area just inside the white region appears to be far whiter. This phenomenon, known as Mach Bands, occurs because various nerves perceiving the pattern are interacting; nerves that lie immediately adjacent to one another tend to inhibit the transmissions of their neighbors, so that the portion of the eye perceiving either the large area of white or of black has a generally lower nerve output than the nerves sensing the borders. These nerves are not inhibited as much, and therefore present far brighter images of the white and black areas.

Sensory masking such as this has its corollary in almost all the senses. In hearing, for example, one frequency is often blocked by tones of another; though both frequencies are vibrating in the cochlea, the nerve transmission from one is masked by the other—usually the higher frequency is blocked while the lower one gets through. A graphic demonstration is what happens on a noisy train when one tries to scream above the din; talking in lower tones than the noise of the train can almost always be understood.

Masking is everywhere evident when it comes to the skin and its tactile/thermal sensory systems. A piece of ice applied to a fiercely itching insect bite helps prevent the release of the itch-producing substance histamine; but it also works at the neurological level by transmitting "cold" messages that help block the transmission of the itch messages. Twinges of muscle pain almost instinctively produce the desire to rub them—to "smooth out" the cramp or knot, but also to provide stimulation that produces lateral inhibition.

Theories of masking and lateral inhibition were also applied to pain, with striking results. In a now-famous experiment, pain induced on a monkey's forearm could be blocked by applying a stimulus to the other side of its arm, causing lateral inhibition and masking the pain.

This type of investigation eventually led to the "pain gate" theory, again reflecting the basic electronic principle of the transistor. Pain gate theory supposed that when the nerve impulses from the various receptors came together at higher levels in the nervous system, only a certain number of impulses could get through the synapse at once since they were all vying for the same space. If the stream of nerve impulses representing pain arrived at the same time as other, broader inputs—such as the touch stimulation provided by vigorously rubbing a banged elbow—then the broader inputs would "close the gate" to further transmission of the pain impulses.

This theory about the body's internal pain relief mechanism eventually led to the development of a technique for externally treating acute pain such as that following surgery. Using a technique known as TENS (Transcutaneous Electrical Nerve Stimulation), an electrode placed near the incision could feed small amounts of electrical stimulation into the nerves leading back to the brain; this was thought not only to block the local transmission of pain at the site of the injury through lateral inhibition, but also to help close the pain gates at higher levels and prevent the pain messages from getting through to the brain.

Acupuncture, too, was originally explained this way—the creation of a stimulus that would block the pain messages by applying a competing stimulus at the synapse. (The real explanation of how acupuncture and TENS work, as we shall see shortly, is infinitely more complex.)

Broadly-tuned nerve receptors working with the Morse code-like signals proposed by the "pattern" theory? A body that could be understood in terms of electronic parts such as transistors and resistors? The explanation was perfect, ideally suited to the logic of the transition period from mechanical to electrical. But society changed yet again in the 1960s, evolving into today's digital era of the computer. And with the change came the realization that the science that had explained the nervous system as a series of electrical circuits had to be revised once again.

The most important part of the new understanding, what characterizes it as belonging to the science of the 1980s, is the emphasis it puts on the brain and spinal cord as the locus of the sensory experience—not on the receptors themselves. In a sense, these "higher order" processing centers in the body are the exact equivalent of a computer's central processing unit—the "brain" where all the various programs are stored that allow the computer's different parts (keyboard, display screen, printers, etc.) to operate.

Even the mechanisms by which the most complex sensory messages are perceived can be understood in terms of a computer's digital processing. A single digital element can be only either + or −, indicating a single bit of binary digital data. But a two-position, two-bit binary "word" can indicate four items of information: + +, + −, − +, − −. With a three-bit word, eight pieces of information can be discriminated, and so forth. Just so, each individual nerve cell can be only either transmitting (on, +) or not (off, −). But when many nerve cells feed into a single neuron, they can form a more complex message composed of the individual cells' on or off states.

Pattern theory's detection of coded, pulselike messages representing the different sensations had been correct; but so was the earlier theory that each type of sensation has its own kind of receptor and separate nerve pathways. Both theories are correct because they explain fundamentally different parts of the nervous system. At the receptor level, indeed, there are different receptors for different sensations, and they are connected to separate nerve pathways. But as the nerve pathways make their way back to the brain some become more and more involved with one another until nerve messages being transmitted close to the brain are indeed composed of the Morse code-like pulses.

As for pain perception itself, the last decade's research has revealed that it not only has an almost completely separate set of nerves from the other tactile and thermal senses, but it itself has four different sets of receptors—nociceptors responsive to noxious (hence their name) heat (burning), pressure (stabbing or cutting), irritation from noxious chemicals, and freezing cold.

Burning, freezing, warmth, cold, itching, irritation, touching, stabbing, etc., etc.—each is sensed at the receptor level by almost completely separate sensory receptors; each could be one of the seventeen senses. Unlike the continuum of frequencies that is perceived as sound, or the continuum of electromagnetic energy that is seen as color, the kind of stimuli perceived by the tactile/thermal/nociceptive nerves are each discrete, each capable of being discriminated and acted on separately. The Renaissance notion that there are but five senses, and but five separate sensory organs to experience them, must finally be exposed as an inadequate explanation and laid to rest.

The most important discoveries about sensory experience of the past two decades have been, as we mentioned, in the area of the role of the brain and spinal cord. But there are also major new findings about the receptors themselves. The perception of pain begins with the stimulation of free nerve endings in the skin whose high firing threshold means that they only respond to potentially damage-causing pressure stimuli. Nothing in the physical configuration of these receptors, it should be noted, has anything to do with how they sense the damage, nor does the shape of any of the other nerve receptors play a role in how *they* sense freezing, cold, burning, etc.

Instead, as with many parts of the nervous system, neural transmitters, which carry messages from one nerve to the next, play a major role. In the case of pain, several neurotransmitters—serotonin, dopamine, and norepinephrine—are involved. Other substances—histamine, prostaglandin, and bradykinin—also released when skin tissue is damaged, both stimulate the pain receptors directly, causing discomfort, and also sensitize the receptors to further stimulation—part of the reason why, for instance, sunburned skin is so sensitive to even mild heating.

These last three substances are also involved in the process of inflammation, which is closely connected with the pain mechanism. At the same time that bradykinin, prostaglandin, and histamine cause the damaged area to swell by causing the constriction of local blood vessels, they interact with each other, resulting in mutual enhancement and making the area particularly sensitive to pain, perhaps in an attempt to keep it from further damage.

With the neural transmitters and related substances uncovered, other very recent research has helped explain some of the actions of common drugs. Aspirin, for example, apparently interferes with the production of prostaglandin, preventing it from sensitizing the nerves and also diminishing the potency of bradykinin. (Prostaglandin is also the substance that enables blood platelets to clot and heal a wound, which is why aspirin can cause microbleeding in some patients.)

The action of anesthetics is also much clearer. Substances such as procaine (sold under the brand name Novocain), lidocaine (sold as Xylocaine), and even cocaine either block local nerve transmission completely by "blocking" the channels through which sodium normally flows into the nerve cell when it is stimulated, or radically interfere with a nerve's ability to transmit high-frequency stimulation patterns—the kind associated with pain. Opiates such as morphine and heroin were initially thought to slow down the responsiveness of nerves in the central nervous system in the same way that anesthetics such as Novocain deaden the peripheral nerves (although, as we shall see, the theory on how opiates work has been subsequently revised).

The discoveries about the role of the central nervous system (CNS)—the brain and spinal cord—are even more fascinating, however. Not one but two very distinct types of neurons carry the stubbed toe message toward the CNS. The first is the quick-acting, insulated kind described earlier—small, efficient nerve fibers, each reserved for a particular kind of pain (if the stubbed toe is burned at the same time, the burn message will be carried along a completely separate nerve fiber).

Impulses travel along these "fast" nerve pathways and reach the spinal cord within milliseconds. Through synapses there they make almost immediate contact with other neurons that send out the signal for instant reflex action: muscle spasms to get the injured part out of the way of further harm; a vascular/breathing spasm that causes one to gasp; and a variety of other signals to visceral organs such as the stomach and groin, leading to the cringing effect (and occasionally nausea).

At the same time that this reflex action is occurring, the same fast-conducting pain nerves make contact with another set of nerves in the spinal cord that carry the pain message along to the lower part of the brain (thalamus) and the brain's cortex itself. The message now initiates additional instinctive responses: increased breathing, increased heartbeat, and increased blood pressure. Finally, the brain issues the message "Pain!" sometimes loudly vocalized, and one feels the stinging, sharp sensation of "first pain."

But while all this is going on, a second set of pain messages, carried over the slower-working, uninsulated nerve fibers that have no additional sheath surrounding them, also arrives at the spinal cord. While the fast-acting neurons each carry only a single kind of pain message, these larger nerve fibers carry information about all types of pain.

At the spinal cord, these larger, slower, uninsulated nerve fibers carrying information about pain form synapses with neurons that are receptive to a whole variety of inputs including pain messages from the small, fast-conducting, insulated pain nerves as well as other stimuli. These "higher order" connections, combining pain with other stimuli, are exactly where those who advocated the pattern theory described earlier had originally made their observations. And the nerves leading away from these synapses do, indeed, show responses to many different types of stimulation that have been "combined" at the synapse, although the nerves leading up to the synapse are far more specific in their sensitivity.

The result is that the "first pain" message carried by the fast-conducting nerves does not usually last longer than the stimulus which caused it. The reflex actions demanded by the injury have already been carried out. Now, unless the damage is severe enough to cause continued "first pain" transmissions, the second wave of impulses will replace the first. A second to a second-and-a-half after the first shock, second pain is felt—dull, aching, annoying, and longer-lasting, but with none of the critical urgency of the first message.

The fast-acting pain nerves are an advantage evolution has given mammals which earlier species lacked; it may be the 1.5-second jump on danger we had that allowed us to survive. First pain tells us quickly where the pain is, how long the stimulus lasted (the nerves keep firing as long as the stimulus lasts), and how strong it was. But first pain subsides quickly, leaving second pain to provide warning signs about truly deep injuries in which there is major damage. It's interesting to note that the inflammation reaction and sensitization involving histamines, prostaglandins, and bradykinin we described earlier affects the "second pain" receptors with their longer-lasting effects whereas these substances have little effect on the "first pain" receptors, which are blocked from further action after the first few moments of injury.

But despite all these advances in knowledge about how the pain receptors work, the most startling new information to have come out of the latest wave of pain research is a profound understanding of the role that the brain itself plays in the pain perception (and pain relief) process.

The mind has always, of course, been suspected of being deeply involved in the perception of pain, and there are many stories about the brain's awesome ability to control what is felt. It is, for instance, a case of "mind over matter" (according to our Western explanations) that allows Indian fakirs to lie on the crushed glass or the religious zealots in voodoo ceremonies to walk on beds of burning coal. The Indian Sun Ceremony also comes to mind—a test of manhood in which the brave skewered himself through the skin of his chest, then tethered himself to a post in the middle of the desert for days.

Many religious experiences, in fact, are associated with this ability to withstand great amounts of pain, often while in the midst of an ecstatic religious trance. The trance can be drug- or alcohol-induced, or it can be brought about simply through the mind's own "power of suggestion" to influence what the body does and doesn't feel. The exalted state also has its parallels in Christianity, where the stories of the martyrs' ability to withstand torture again attest to the "miraculous" power that the mind can have. Buddhist meditation is another form of the same phenomenon, a "natural high" in which the body is somehow removed from its surroundings and numbed to the effects of pain.

It is undoubtedly the same process that accounts for the seeming desensitization to ordinary pain that is sometimes experienced during sex, so that we perceive as pleasurable what might normally be considered excruciatingly painful. The exact mechanism is still somewhat unclear, but it may have to do with some process of lateral inhibition in which the sexual stimulation masks many of the ordinary pain inputs. Or it may have to do with the same mechanisms that cause the religious experiences noted above.

In schizophrenics, whose powers of visual, auditory, and olfactory perception are distorted, it is not surprising to find that pain perception is affected quite dramatically. There are stories of schizophrenics with perforated ulcers, badly broken bones, acute appendicitis, and even heart attacks who reported feeling absolutely no pain. Not only weren't they conscious of the pain stimulus, but their bodies showed none of the instinctual responses normally associated with pain.

There is also obviously an important connection between mental processes and the relief of pain. When Indian medicine men and shamans in many other cultures go to work on a patient, only part of their often amazing powers are derived from the various drugs and remedies they use. The medicine man "believes" that he can cure the patient, and the patient believes he can be cured. When the shaman, following rituals prescribed by generations of his ancestors, "sucks the disease" out of the patient, displays it as a small oblong object, then throws it into the fire, both patient and medicine man accept that the disease has been removed; in some cases, the patient is as likely to recover as if he had been treated by surgery.

The psychological factors in pain relief are actually among modern medicine's most potent weapons against pain. Being distracted from thinking about a pain may be enough to help forget it's there —as can be readily demonstrated by giving a new toy to a baby with teething pain. Simple distraction may be all that is involved when dentists play loud rock and roll music while performing anesthetic-free drilling.

Emotions certainly affect pain perception. If the body is tense and the mind anxious, pain will almost certainly be worse. One highly-effective technique for pain relief is therefore simple relaxation—either self-induced or suggested by another. One therapist's method is to suggest that the patient imagine him or herself a rag doll filled with sand. The therapist touches the patient close to the injured area and tells the patient to imagine that all the sand is running out of that area. Now touching other parts, the therapist tells the patient to imagine that all the sand is running out. As the imaginary sand runs out, so does the patient's anxiety and the pain.

Biofeedback can have much the same results, with the small electronic beeper set to monitor the patient's blood pressure, skin moisture, and so forth. By deliberately slowing the heartbeat, lowering blood pressure, and preventing tension from building, the person connected with a biofeedback machine can often prevent his or her own pain.

Then, of course, there is the "placebo effect," in which administration of sugar pills made up to look like real medicine, or injections of harmless saline solution, can sometimes produce the same pain-killing effects as a real drug—even on relatively severe pain such as that following wisdom tooth extraction. It's easy to laugh off as psychosomatic someone's pain when it is relieved by placebos; but tooth pain is very real, and the placebos *do* work.

Still another brain-based curing process is evident in hypnosis, where the brain's pain-sensing mechanism can apparently be "turned off" so that sticking a needle in a hypnotized subject's arm elicits none of the instinctual responses normally associated with pain. The hypnotist can also, through suggestion, help prevent a patient from feeling pain from conditions such as arthritis after the patient has awakened. Conversely, the hypnotist can suggest, experimentally, that the patient is feeling or will feel extreme pain; the results, in terms of the body's reflex systems, are the same as if the stimulus were real.

There is also another widely observed effect in hypnosis that may prove to have profound significance in pain research. Although the hypnotic patient's *body* can be desensitized to pain so that the various reflex responses are blocked, something in the subject's mind remains alert—a "hidden observer" that watches out for the patient. After experimental painful stimuli were applied while in a trance, patients reported that although they felt no actual pain, they knew something was wrong. The "hidden observer," acting on a different cognitive level than the actual pain perception center, was aware that there was potential danger. It is interesting to speculate whether the "hidden observer" would wake the patient from the trance if the experiment could be allowed to continue to the point where there was actual tissue damage.

All these various effects of the relationship between the brain and the pain perception/blocking mechanism—hypnosis, placebos, religious ecstasy, relaxation, and the rest—have been known about for some time, of course. The most exciting discovery in pain research, however, has come in defining the exact biochemical nature of this relationship—how, in fact, the brain's own chemistry influences the perception of pain stimuli. The discovery came as recently as 1975. Researchers looking into the effects that morphine has on the body discovered that they had been wrong in the assumption that morphine simply anesthetizes nerves in the central nervous system in the same way that substances such as Novocain deaden the peripheral nerves. If morphine was an anesthetic, why didn't it also prevent the nerve impulses that produced muscular activity (it plainly doesn't)?

The answer for morphine, and for the other opiates, is that they actually stimulate part of the nervous system rather than suppressing it. This turns out to be the key discovery that has led to the current theory of pain and its relief. In a complex process, morphine, attracted to opiate receptor sites in the brain, stimulates serotonin-utilizing nerves descending from the brain down the spinal cord. Impulses from these nerves inhibit pain impulses traveling toward the brain, thus "turning off" or decreasing the perception of pain.

But the morphine research has gone even further. It has been discovered that the chemists who discovered morphine back in the seventeenth century had accidentally duplicated a substance found in the body itself—endorphins, a group of internally produced opiates. In other words, morphine actually mimics the body's own pain-suppressing chemicals.

It turns out that as pain messages are received by the spinal cord and sent along to the brain, the brain's endorphins respond by activating the descending serotonin pathways (and perhaps other inhibitory pathways as well), preventing further pain messages from getting through. Thus, the brain itself is the body's number-one pain-killing mechanism.

Do the various "psychological" pain cures—such as the placebo effect or the medicine man—actually cause the body to release endorphins and therefore reduce pain? Fortunately, there is a simple method to see whether an opiate (either injected or produced internally) is involved in reducing pain; an injection of the substance naloxone prevents the opiate from working by occupying the "opiate receptor sites" and thereby preventing the opiate from exerting its influence. Therefore, if endorphins are responsible for reducing or eliminating pain in a particular situation, an injection of naloxone should, by counteracting the endorphins, cause the pain to be felt almost immediately.

And this, indeed, is proving to be the case in experiment after experiment. Schizophrenics injected with naloxone begin to feel pain again. Those reporting relief with placebos no longer feel relief when naloxone is injected. And it would not be surprising if it turned out that patients being treated by relaxation therapy, or by shamans and medicine men, did not also find the results reversed by naloxone injections.

Perhaps the biggest evidence of all has come from the amazing pain-prevention and relief of acupuncture and acupressure. Amazingly enough, the early Chinese doctors who developed the techniques described how the needle insertions produced "fluids" that ran through the body and caused the pain to abate, very strongly suggesting what we now think to be the explanation of how it works.

First, it must be pointed out that even the Chinese themselves no longer accept the early view on acupuncture that the needles had to be inserted along the twelve meridian lines—that a needle stuck in the foot would be more effective in curing back pain than a needle in the arm. The most widely-used practice currently is to insert the needles either in the skin close to the part that hurts or else close to the main nerve line carrying information about that part back to the brain. In this way, simple lateral inhibition between the pain-carrying nerves and the nerves stimulated by the acupuncture will help cancel out some of the pain messages.

But the real value of the needles is in stimulating the brain to release endorphins, which in turn stimulate the production of serotonin, and activate descending inhibitory impulses which in turn prevent pain messages from being conducted in the spinal cord and brain. To prove the theory, injections with naloxone reverse the analgesic (pain-killing) effects of the acupuncture treatment. Western medicine, which for so long rejected the idea that acupuncture could possibly be effective, can take some satisfaction in the knowledge that its research provided the neurophysiological explanation of how the acupuncture process works.

Of course, as we have made clear so many times throughout this discussion, it must be remembered that the current explanation is merely the one that satisfies our current need to know. Already, not more than eight years after endorphins were discovered, it is being suggested that several other brain-centered mechanisms may also be responsible for pain perception and reduction. Pain relief from hypnosis, for instance, is *not* reversed by naloxone, suggesting that both the "hidden observer" and the process by which hypnotism reduces pain may be completely separate pain-sensing mechanisms. This also goes along with some studies on acupuncture that show that although acupuncture is quite effective in reducing the sensory experience of pain, it has far less effect on the emotional part—so that those receiving acupuncture still seem to react emotionally to the pain stimulus even though they may feel no "physical" discomfort.

Other pain relief pathways are also being discovered—those that result from the blocking effect caused by other pain. In these experiments, when a painful shock is applied to an animal's foot, pain from another part of the body will be blocked. It is doubtful that simple lateral inhibition is responsible, since it is unlikely that nerves from the foot converge with nerves from other, distant body parts. But endorphins are not the answer, either, since naloxone has no effect.

Besides the research going on in alternate pain pathways, there is also considerable attention being paid again to the skin receptors. As much as is known, we still aren't certain why some receptors are sensitive to burning, some to freezing, some to cutting, and so forth. The next wave of scientific research may, in fact, prove that some other chemical substance produced by the brain "predisposes" a receptor to respond to a particular stimulus. Research hasn't even started in this direction yet, but when one looks at the pendulum effect that has gone on in pain research, the continual swing back and forth between looking at the skin receptors, then the higher order processes, then the skin receptors and higher order processes again, it would not be surprising to find scientists reinvestigating the receptor level to once again push back the boundaries of knowledge in that area too.

But, for the moment, endorphins and their effect on serotonin pathways remain the "ultimate answer"—with a very real manifestation in everyday life. There are very few women who would not agree that delivering a child is probably the most painful experience of their lives. It is fascinating to note, therefore, that the body does something about it; endorphin levels actually build steadily during the course of the pregnancy until they reach extremely high levels just before labor. The human body apparently doesn't subscribe to the notion that the pain of childbirth is just "nature's way."

What's more, the body may also get the future mother's assistance in building the endorphin reserve whether she likes it or even knows about it or not. Pickles and ice cream? Strange food tastes? It's been known for some time that the body demands foods that are necessary to keep the baby healthy and growing. But some of these foods, known to be high in substances necessary for serotonin production, may be for Mom herself—to build up her internal pain-killing abilities in preparation for the pain of giving birth.

Chapter Three
Two Different Worlds...

Double, double toil and trouble;
Fire burn, and cauldron bubble.
Fillet of a fenny snake,
In the cauldron boil and bake;
Eye of newt and toe of frog,
Wool of bat and tongue of dog,
Adder's fork and blind-worm's sting,
Lizard's leg and howlet's wing....

William Shakespeare, MACBETH

The thick flaps covering the lizard's narrow, slit-like eyes rolled back slowly, exposing blood-red orbs to the full glare of the noonday sun. The eyes roved about aimlessly, fixing on one thing and then another but never at the same time, the brain processing the incoming data separately to form two hazy, flat images. There was nothing moving—which was all the detail that the eyes could report, but all the lizard needed to know. Nearby a plant with spiny thorns had bloomed, sending forth flowers of magnificent yellows and oranges; but it was insignificant to the lizard's destiny, and if its eyes saw a murky gray and white image of the flowers, its brain paid them no heed.

A similar set of findings was produced by its ears—two purplish drum-like membranes stretched across its head just behind the jaw. Somewhere off in the far distance a large creature was walking about, causing the ground to vibrate slightly. This it was able to detect.

Otherwise, for the lizard, the place was still; the insects chirping in a nearby bush produced sounds that its hearing membranes could not detect.

But today there *was* something special in the air—something different. The lizard's tongue explored the ground for telltale signs. A small rat-like animal had passed by several hours ago, followed a little later by a larger furry animal—probably in pursuit of the first. Others, like the lizard itself in size and shape, had also been present; an old, large member of a closely-related species left a particularly distasteful odor, and the lizard backed away from it. In the air there was the scent of fresh water, perhaps a mile away to the southwest.

Meanwhile the sun was getting higher in the sky, its rays now almost directly overhead. The chemical change inside the lizard's body was dramatic as the small "third eye" in the middle of its forehead responded to the sun's rays as if he had actually seen them. Suddenly it was time to seek cover—to get out of the sun before its body temperature became too high (though it would never actually feel the variations as temperature until it reached the point when it would sear its skin). Using the sun's rays this time as a navigation guide, it flicked out its tongue once more and sensed the presence of its burrow nearby. It began walking toward it.

Suddenly it stopped, flicking out its tongue furiously, its eyes darting about madly. Then, in an instant, it sensed what the "special something in the air" was—a great bird of prey sitting on the log just outside its burrow entrance.

Staunchly the lizard raised itself up on its four legs, hissing at the bird. But the bird began beating its wings, then suddenly darted out with its talons at the lizard's body. The lizard could do nothing except fight, and swinging its long tail, whipped it into the bird's face. The bird squawked furiously at the pain, but it only became more insistent. Viciously the bird grasped for the lizard's tail.

The lizard felt the talons digging into the flesh of its tail—there was no pain as there would have been if the talons had penetrated its body, but simply the sensation of being touched. This moment was critical. Struggling against the bird's fierce grip, the lizard suddenly felt its tail snap off. Quickly it raced into its burrow, down into the coolness of the earth. A few moments later the wound at the base of its spine healed over. Within a few months it would have grown back into a tail again. Meanwhile, the lizard was still alive, while the bird of prey was left holding a still-wriggling but useless tail. . . .

This account is so strange it might as well be science fiction, though it actually describes a rather commonplace day in the life of several lizard species living in the desert of Arizona. The strangeness arises because, for all intents and purposes, these reptiles inhabit a world totally different from that of humans. Some of the features are the same, of course, as they are between the moon and the earth. But the creature's sensory systems are so different from ours, responsive to so different a slice of the continuum of nature, that they could as easily be living on a different planet.

The eye of the horsefly is divided into some 20,000 individual eye cell clusters, each responding to either electromagnetic radiation of highly specific wavelengths or else a specific chemical molecule in the air, combining the input from all its receptors into a still not clearly understood "image" of the environment. Does this creature really exist in the same world with us?

The difference between man and lizard, between man and most other species, comes down to the simple fact that each species not only perceives different portions of the total continuum of nature, but also perceives the same pieces of the continuum differently. This is true for chemical stimuli—what we define as taste and smell —and, equally, for mechanical stimuli such as touch and temperature. But most especially it applies to electromagnetic stimuli in the range of sight and sound to which humans respond.

The grounds for the difference lie in the tremendous expanse of the electromagnetic spectrum itself. The electromagnetic spectrum encompasses wave-like energy with a range of wavelengths and frequencies (cycles per second) that increases some 100,000,000,000,000,000,000,000 times from smallest to largest. It stretches all the way from the energy that represents the resonating frequency of the earth—approximately .001 cycles per second (one cycle every 16½ minutes), with wavelengths around 100,000,000,000 (10^{11}) meters—roughly the distance from the earth to the sun—all the way to the energy represented by secondary cosmic rays, such as the photons produced by solar flare-ups, vibrating at a rate of 10,000,000,000,000,000,000,000 cycles per second (10^{16} megaherz) with a wavelength of only .000000000001 centimeters (10^{-4} angstroms*), corresponding roughly to the diameter of an electron.

If each power of ten of wavelength and frequency were arbitrarily measured as an inch, and the total length of the spectrum therefore measured about 26 inches, the total amount of spectrum that can be perceived by the human eye represents less than a quarter of an inch, with sensitivity from around 400 nanometers** (perceived as deep blue) to around 700 nanometers (perceived as deep red). Below this, as wavelengths lengthen and frequency decreases, there is a narrow band of energy we perceive as body heat. Lower still, separated by the energy used to transmit radio and television signals, is the minuscule amount of spectrum space we can perceive as sound—energy from about 20 to 20,000 cycles per second. Just below the visual spectrum is the energy that causes suntanning and kills germs—ultraviolet light. Even further up and down the spectral scale are the energy forms that constitute radar signals, molecular and radioactive energy, brain wave frequencies, electrical power, and so forth.

It should come as no surprise, therefore, to discover that not all species have sensory systems tuned to exactly the same portions of the electromagnetic spectrum that ours are. For example, though humans are "blind" to most ultraviolet light (to the point where the retina can be damaged by staring at an ultraviolet light source that is apparently dark), other species can perceive it directly and use their perceptions for foodgathering, mating, direction finding, and so on, in the same way humans use vision and hearing.

An example are bees, whose basic process of color vision is re-

---

* One angstrom equals one hundred-millionth of a centimeter.
** One nanometer equals one billionth of a meter.

markably similar to man's (although it evolved quite separately). Both bees and humans have color vision based on three different kinds of cells responsive to three different wavelengths of light—the primary colors out of which every other color is composed. The difference between the two, however, is that while human sensitivity is greatest to red, green, and blue colors, bee eye cells are most sensitive to yellow, blue, and ultraviolet.

In this scheme, bees are all but insensitive to red, and since purple is a mixture of the two extremes of the visible spectrum (red and violet for humans), "bee purple" is different from "human purple," being a mixture of yellow and ultraviolet. White, too, is a different color for bees since the combination of spectral colors that make up white in the human world is different in the world of bees. Most significant of all, of course, is that flowers take on a completely different appearance once ultraviolet reflectance values are added in. The red in flowers is essentially invisible to bees; but because different parts of a bloom may reflect ultraviolet light, most flowers are not only visible but also patterned to bees, often indicating the presence of nectar. And what might be considered similar in human perception—two red flowers, for example—is probably perceived by the bee as differently as red and green might be for us.

Since sensory systems reflect the particular needs of the organism in the environment, it would actually be surprising to find that sensory systems did not differ widely. In fifty million years of evolving to meet the continually shifting environment, nature has indeed produced an astonishing variety of sensory systems, as diverse as the species themselves.

It is even possible to recognize the sensory systems of plants. Trees grow toward the sun because "growth substances" have been produced in response to the environmental stimulus. Similarly, when a plant grows leaves in the spring, it is responding directly to the angle of the sun's rays and its own internal clock. A new discovery is that some trees may even be able to signal each other, so their sensitivity is not only to the environment but also to other trees. When infested by tent caterpillars, willow trees release a substance in their leaves that makes the insects grow more slowly. Surprisingly, uninfested willows nearby also begin to produce this defensive substance, seemingly in response to some message emitted by the trees under attack. Since the trees are often separated by considerable distances, the signal is probably an airborne chemical carried from tree to tree by breezes.

There is indeed some truth to the notion that house plants will respond favorably if they hear music or are talked and sung to regularly. The sonic vibrations appear to be absorbed by the plants in the same way as light rays, and the mechanical energy of the sound used to stimulate the production of growth hormones. The only mystery in this process is why plants "need" such a sensory ability.

Some of the differences between human senses and those of other species are merely extensions of what we already know—super-refined hearing, for example, which allows predators to stalk their victims in the dark, or the insect's compound eye, which gives it a multifaceted image of the world, or the tongue of the lizard, that enables it to detect highly complex tastes and smells given off by potential mates.

A classic example is the barn owl, which is able to pinpoint precisely the minute sounds made by small mice (its prey) from high overhead. According to the latest studies, made by actually measuring the owl's brain waves as it tracks experimental targets, the owl is able to use its hearing to tell not only the direction but also the distance of the sounds it hears better than any other living species tested.

It does this by the relatively simple biological adaptation of having its two ears slightly asymmetrical, with one pointed more upward and the other more downward. This accentuates a phenomenon present to some extent in humans: the fact that sound reaches the two different ears at slightly different times and with slightly different volumes. In humans this accounts for the ability to tell, generally, from which direction a sound came. But in owls, extremely rapid calculation of the difference between the sound reaching the left ear and the right, both in strength (loudness) and also in timing (one arrives a little ahead of the other), enables the owl to calculate the exact location of its prey and also its elevation (in other words, how far above its prey the owl is).

On the ground, of course, the prey is not completely without defenses of its own. In the case of the kangaroo rat, a small nocturnal rodent that lives in desert areas, its two main enemies are the rattlesnake, with its unique heat-sensing ability, and the owl, with its offset-ear-triangulation hearing, more precise than electronic radar. In defense, the kangaroo rat has developed greatly enlarged middle ear cavities, giving it extrasensitive hearing in the low frequency (1000–3000 cycles) range. As the owl swoops down toward the rat, the rodent's ears pick up and amplify the low (1200 cycles) whirring sound produced by the owl's wing beats (which can be detected by humans only after considerable electronic amplification). Then, just as the owl is about to strike, the tiny kangaroo rat earns its name by making a spectacular upward leap, landing at least a foot away from where the owl is striking.

Kangaroo rats avoid the rattlesnake in much the same way, making no attempt to escape while the snake is preparing to strike. Just as surely as it avoids the owl, however, the rat responds to a barely audible sound (at around 2000 cycles) made just as the snake initiates its final move. Scientists still are not sure about the nature of the sound—perhaps a hiss, or a rattle, or the snake's scales moving against the ground—but they save the kangaroo rat's life almost every time. Interestingly, several other nocturnal animals that live in desert-like environments—including gerbils and jerboas—have the same kind of inner ear cavity enlargement (and the large hindquarters necessary for them to spring away), indicating that they, too, may possess enhanced hearing in the low-frequency range.

Human hearing is nowhere near as refined. But in the human animal—a basically diurnal (daylight-living) species—hearing is not nearly as important as seeing—which is developed in humans as an extremely precise sensory system, able to detect not only forms (the way light is reflected off objects), but also colors (the particular wavelengths of the light). This is presumably in response to the needs of the species to be able to differentiate various food substances, among many other uses.

Different again is the "hearing" ability of bats which enables them to use ultrasonic, radar-like sound transmission/reception completely outside the range of human hearing, to echolocate around obstacles and catch prey on the wing. The most remarkable feature of this sensory apparatus is that highly specific information about the presence, distance, direction, and nature of distant objects, equivalent to that obtained by most animals through vision, can be determined by bats simply from echoes.

Among bats there are actually two very different types of echolocation schemes. The simpler of the two uses pulses not at all unlike the frequency modulation technique of FM radio (in which a basic wave pattern is contoured according to the pitch of the transmitted sound). Bats using this technique emit a stream of extremely brief frequency modulated auditory pulses that sweep downward through an entire octave within five milliseconds. By comparing the difference between the emitted sound and the returning echo, the bat's brain is able to make split-second determinations about what lies ahead precisely in the same way as radar or sonar. Distance between the bat and an object is probably determined by measuring the time that elapses between the outgoing sound and the returning echo. The size of the target can be calculated by comparison of how the different frequencies in the emitted burst are reflected back. And the direction of the target is probably determined by binaural comparisons of intensities of different frequencies in the echo—in much the same way as barn owls and humans, but using a different kind of signal.

The other kind of bat echolocation uses brief bursts of a constant wavelength of sound in addition to the method described above. Bats that use this second kind of echolocation apparently have an internal Doppler shift calculator that allows them to align themselves on a target based on how the constant pitch is reflected by the object. (The Doppler effect, indicating the relative distance of two objects from one another, accounts for the changing pitch of a train whistle as it approaches and then moves away from the listener.)

The key to this echolocation system is that the bat's hearing is most sensitive in the range 1000-3000 cycles higher than the sound emitted by its vocal cords. The difference between the emitted frequency (to which the bat's hearing is not that sensitive) and the frequency of maximum hearing sensitivity corresponds exactly to the amount of Doppler shift that is caused by an object directly in front of the bat when flying at its typical flight speed. Objects not directly in front of the bat return echoes that fall outside this range of maximum hearing sensitivity. In other words, by tuning into the most clearly defined echo signals, the bat is able to both avoid objects immediately in front of it and also follow objects through the sky. This Doppler shift information can be used, like the FM pulses described in the first kind of bat echolocation, to provide extremely precise information about objects, including the relative speeds of bat and target and the target's precise angle.

Echolocation may also account for how marine mammals such as porpoises and perhaps whales, seals, and sea lions find their way about in the ocean's depth—and may account for their almost constant vocalizations which, like the frequency modulation pulses of bats, are constantly changing in pitch and appear to be sweeping the spectrum.

Another sensory system with absolutely no human equivalent is the recently discovered ability of some snakes to actually "see" the heat patterns given off by other animals—particularly their warm-blooded prey. The snake's infrared sensing mechanism is so accurate it can lead the snake to a perfect, venomous strike on a completely dark night—as accurately as the snake performs in the daytime. The infrared sensing ability not only helps the snake "see" its victim in the dark, but also allows the snake to detect the distance and direction of warm-blooded objects from quite far away.

The sense organ used for infrared sensing by rattlers, other pit vipers such as cottonmouths and copperheads, and the boid snake family (including snakes such as the python), is a cavity on the surface of the head. Two of these cavities, or pits, are located just under the eyes in rattlers, and thirteen pairs line the jaws of boid snakes. Inside the pit, a sense organ as well-defined as the human ear or eye, is a membrane on which is arranged the rich network of sensory nerve endings that can respond to changes in temperature. The slightest hint of warmth, as little as three-thousandths of a degree, stimulates the nerve endings to transmit messages to the brain. Because the opening of the pit is small, and the incoming heat information is directed toward a specific part of the membrane, the snake can tell from what angle the source of infrared illumination came.

In many ways this infrared sensing ability is similar to the human process of vision, except that in the snake the nerve fibers carrying the infrared information do not travel along the same pathways as optical information. Instead, they form a separate, parallel system to vision, traveling along the same nerve fibers which in humans carry tactile information (touch, warmth, pain, etc.) from the facial region back to the brain.

Once inside the brain, however, information from the snake's eyes and its pit organs is combined into a unique type of vision in which the snake literally sees the infrared patterns of its prey as clearly as we see its colors. In the same portion of the brain that in humans is reserved for vision, nerve impulses from the pits and the eyes are combined. Just as the human process of vision is arranged so that the visual center in the brain is like a map of the external world, with each sector of the visual field provided with its own corresponding sector in the visual cortex (see Chapter 1), so the nerve cells from the snake's eyes and the pit organ are also organized to provide a map corresponding to the environment.

This organization of the snake's brain is found nowhere else. In the processing of the information, visual and infrared nerve fibers interact by combining into more complex nerve cells that react differently when differing amounts of visual and infrared information are present, sometimes favoring the infrared data, sometimes the visual data, and sometimes actually combining the two into a single image. The net result is that the snake actually "sees" the object emitting the infrared radiation.

The ability to sense heat is also found, of course, in humans, but it takes a considerable amount of radiant energy to warm the various layers of skin lying on top of human warmth-sensing cells. The heat receptors of the snake's pit organ, on the other hand, are located in a membrane only 15 micrometers thick, so it takes only about one twentieth as much heat to excite these nerve cells as it does to stimulate human heat receptors.

Yet another "alien" sensory system coming to light now that science has begun looking outside the individual boundaries of human perception, is the ability of several different kinds of organisms to sense the earth's magnetic fields. This ability is found in creatures as small as bacteria, whose bodies contain small particles of iron oxide (or magnetite) that they synthesize out of naturally occurring soluble iron. The particles, organized in a row down the length of each bacterium, transform the organism into a biological magnet that can orient itself along the polar axes even after it has died.

The interesting part is that some bacteria are magnetized so their heads point in a northerly direction, and some so their heads point south. Apparently this is related to the fact that these bacteria thrive in an environment where there is very little or no oxygen—down in the mud and sediment at the bottom of the ocean. Because of the direction of the magnetic field, in the northern hemisphere, the northward-magnetized bacteria automatically head down deeper into the sediment (and toward the pole). In the southern hemisphere, this is reversed and it is the south-seeking bacteria that head down, toward the pole. Since the geomagnetic field at the equator is horizontal, both north and south-seeking bacteria are directed horizontally here. While neither group is directed toward the sediment, the magnetic sensing ability does help keep these bacteria away from the potentially lethal oxygen levels in the upper layers of the ocean bottom.

This ability to sense magnetic fields is not limited to bacteria; the same kind of iron oxide synthesized by the bacteria is also present within the brains of certain bird species, which can apparently detect the earth's magnetic fields as an aid to navigation and migration. There is no doubt, of course, that birds rely heavily on visual cues—landmarks, or the position of the sun or the stars—as their major method of orientation. But when visual cues are not present—such as on nights when cloud cover prevents the birds from seeing the ground below and the stars overhead—how do the birds navigate? Some species such as the homing pigeon apparently do orient themselves by means of magnetic field detectors.

In one experiment, an electromagnet is placed on a homing pigeon's head so that the magnetic environment can be distorted. When the bird is allowed to see the sun, it will orient itself correctly in the direction home, no matter what the polarity of the electromagnet. But when it is prevented from seeing the sun, its magnetic sense takes over and it will misorient itself according to the polarity of the electromagnet.

This use of magnetic fields for orientation is essential to successful migrations. If a robin is prevented from seeing external cues and placed in a special cage in which the magnetic field surrounding the cage can be controlled, it orients itself according to the artificial field. If the electromagnetic field is weakened to a level below the earth's own normal force, however, the bird can no longer orient itself properly.

The artificial field is also used to prove that it is not the north/south orientation of the magnetic field but rather its position relative to the horizon that the robins use most readily. Reversing the polarity of the field still results in correct orientation, whereas reversing the angle from below horizon to above horizon results in a 180 degree misorientation.

Clues to understanding the mechanism for this magnetic sensitivity have actually come quite recently, from a mammalian species some consider quite close to man: the dolphin. Scientists have discovered, located between the brain and the skull of the common Pacific dolphin, specialized tissue containing the same form of iron oxide (magnetite) found in magnetically sensitive bacteria and birds. The tissue containing the magnetite is attached by a stalk to a network of active nerve fibers—now all thought to be part of a sensory system that responds to magnetic changes. One possible explanation of how the system works is that although it is unlikely that the magnetite is permanently magnetized in one pole or the other, the tissue is sensitive enough to emit a pulse of nerve energy when changing from one magnetic orientation to another. Another theory is that the magnetite tissue deforms slightly as the animal crosses magnetic fields, setting up a nerve impulse response.

It has not yet been proven that these dolphins use the magnetic sensitivity for migration or home-seeking, nor even that the magnetic-sensing cells actually function to detect changes in the magnetic fields. But research is definitely leading in this direction, and also toward the possibility that humans, too, possess magnetic sensitivity.

The point in all of this is not simply to show the diversity of nature. Rather, our concern is to demonstrate that each individual species and organism accurately reflects the particular aspects of the environment that it needs to survive. In the development of night-hunting species such as the pit viper snakes, infrared sensing is obviously a critical factor in determining the presence of potential prey. On the other hand, the ability to discriminate color is a far more useful sense for diurnal species such as man. The logical extension of this is the somewhat heretical notion that we might come to a better understanding of the world in which an organism lives—in other words, the section of the world of which it partakes through its sensory apparatus—by studying its sensory systems themselves and their particular sensitivities. Carrying this idea one step further, the universe according to man becomes far more defined in its limitations once it is understood that we only perceive a very small portion of the whole.

Magnetic fields, infrared radiation, and high-pitched sounds are just the beginning when it comes to portions of nature's continuum the human senses cannot detect. Another important area of the electromagnetic spectrum for which we apparently have no sense organ is ordinary electricity. Humans can, of course, experience electrical energy directly, as with electrical shock; but in that case the electrical energy is flowing directly through the body and stimulating the central nervous system directly. For organisms with electrical detecting ability, however, there is a sensory system as well developed as the human eye or ear.

Electrical and electromagnetic forces are especially evident in

water—both salt and fresh. Humans, of course, have no sensitivity to them, but weak electric fields are given off by many underwater species. Many inanimate objects also create electricity, caused by the interaction of their structural materials with the water—as happens in a car battery. In most cases these electrical fields take the form of direct current (DC) voltage, in which the electrons that determine the charge are always flowing in one direction. In salt water the charge can range from one hundred millionth of a volt per centimeter to one hundred thousandth of a volt per centimeter.

Alternating current (AC) voltage, the kind found in standard household lines where the polarity of the current (or the direction of the electron flow) changes sixty times a second, occurs more rarely, and is usually associated with the movements of various aquatic organisms that set up the regular electrical cycles.

Plainly, any organism that could detect these minute quantities of electricity would be at a considerable advantage. Electricity moves in water at almost the speed of light, providing far more rapid information than auditory or chemical signals, which travel slowly in water. Electricity would also enable fish to "see" in darkness, or when visual cues were blocked. Thus, it turns out that a number of aquatic organisms have evolved specialized receptors with which they can perceive many aspects of the underwater electrical world.

In some instances, the ability to detect electrical signals is passive, in the sense that the fish simply receives messages being given off by other organisms or the environment. Sharks, for instance, are thought to be able to detect their prey by sensing thrashing or swimming movements in the water as relatively strong low-frequency electrical signals. There are two groups of unrelated freshwater fishes, however, that have evolved not only specialized sensory systems that detect minute amounts of electricity in the water but also specialized organs capable of generating electric discharges which are used like a bat's echolocation signals. The electric discharge is produced by an organ that may have evolved from muscle groups in the fish's eye and tail whose nerve cells discharge their electricity into the water rather than stimulating the muscle. The electric organ discharge (EOD) is similar to the extremely strong current produced by electric eels (up to several hundred volts) that is used to stun prey.

In the two groups of fishes that use electrical discharges as an aid in navigation, the EOD is much weaker than the discharges of eels. In one group, the South American knifefish, the electric organ runs almost the entire length of the body. In the other, the mormyrids, the electric organ is almost always in the tail. Each time an EOD occurs, an electric field spreads out from the fish's body, and objects whose electrical properties are different from the water, such as a rock or another fish, will distort the EOD field.

To sense the distortion patterns, these fish have receptors scattered across the body surface. The distorted, reflected EOD will therefore stimulate the receptors at some locations more than others, creating an electrical image of the object in the environment on the fish's body surface.

To enhance this electrical image, fishes have also evolved a way of focusing the EOD reflections. Some, for example, use their electric organ-containing tails to explore new features of the environment, backing in tail first to get a "closer look." Other species focus their electroreceptive abilities by swimming rapidly backward and forward along an object and increasing their EOD rate, thus maximizing the amount of information being provided to the electroreceptors.

In addition to the use of electroreception for navigation, one theory is that it can also play a role in migration. Electroreceptive fish which also migrate could learn and remember the electric images cast on its body during migration as an aid in long-range orientation.

This profound difference in sensitivity between humans and fish is present in all the sensory systems. Human vision, for instance, has a central visual field in front of each eye, and peripheral vision extending out to the sides. Except for some minor differences in color sensitivity between the center of the visual field and the periphery, however, color vision is uniform throughout the eye and objects in any part of the visual field can be distinguished from the background with equal clarity. For fish, however, water does not present a uniform color environment, and their color vision provides information that not only distinguishes one object from another but also helps establish which way is up, which way to school with other fish, and so forth.

The difference between human and fish color vision arises from a difference in the environment itself. For humans and most other terrestrial species, a primary function of vision is to tell the difference between a foreground object and the background, particularly by comparing and contrasting the colors of the two. In water, however, the background and the foreground object often appear the same color since, because of light scattering, the water itself is differently colored in different directions. In addition, substances in the water such as dissolved organic matter from decaying plants, microscopic organisms, and so forth affect the absorption of different wavelengths. Therefore, another means besides human-type color vision has evolved to enable fish to separate objects such as prey fish and predators from the surrounding water.

Because the surrounding water has such different colors, the visual systems of fish have had to adapt to water's specific qualities. For example, those species that live in the depth of the ocean where there is very little light generally have rod cell pigments in the eye that closely match the deep blue color of the water at that depth (the rod cell pigments in humans, used to detect lightness and darkness, are not really sensitive to color). Since the only way the objects that represent the fish's prey can be seen is by the light they reflect, and since they are darker (reflect less light) than the general background, having eye pigments matched to the color of the water allows the fish to perceive their prey objects as darker than the background. Fish that live closer to the surface, however, where there is generally more light, have rod cell pigments that are shifted away from the color of the water. In this way, the background water color is not perceived nearly as sharply as the lighter colors of the prey objects.

The same kind of differentiation occurs in the cone cells, which produce color vision. Pigments in these cells are matched to the specific habitats of the species, offering them optimal vision in their particular habitat within the environment.

Not all fish have cone cells in the retina. Fish with cone cells generally live closer to the surface than those with rod cells alone, since it takes a great deal more light to stimulate the cones than the rods. Moreover, since water progressively filters out more and more of light's wavelengths (first red, then green and yellow, finally leaving only deep blue), fish that live at the bottom would find no use for color vision in a monochromatic environment in which only blue can be perceived. Fish living closer to the surface, however, exist in an environment in which there are many more wavelengths in the light.

Within this multicolored environment there has been considerable adaptation to the specific qualities of the water. Fish that are active near the surface at dawn or dusk when the light has a reddish quality, and which during the day inhabit slightly deeper water that also allows red wavelengths as well as green to penetrate, often have green- and red-sensitive cone pigments but lack blue-sensitive chemicals. Fish that live in murky water have adapted by developing three types of cone cells, all attuned to the longer wavelengths which are all that can penetrate this environment.

Water color is not the only determining factor in the pigmentation of the cone cells, however. In the case of fish that dwell exclusively just under the surface, where a large amount of light penetrates without a great deal of wavelength absorption by the water, many species have three cone pigments, similar to the red-, green-, and blue-sensitive arrangement of human cones, except that here the pigments are most sensitive to violet, blue-green, and yellow-green. The pigments for sensing red, even though red wavelengths are still visible, are almost entirely absent.

A special case of this type of fish is the guppy, which has two separate retinas in each eye. Because of the way the lens of the guppy's eye focuses incoming images, the lower retina receives light from above; it contains green-sensitive cones almost exclusively so that when the guppy is looking upward it can easily pick out dark bits of food contrasted against the light background. The top retina, however, which receives light from down below and in front of the fish, contains three different kinds of cone cells in an arrangement like the human eye, capable of true color vision. Presumably, this allows the guppy to pick out predators swimming toward it from down below. Significantly, when male guppies perform their ritual courtship display and flash their brightly colored tails, they do so from a position just slightly below and in front of the female guppy's face.

Nothing better illustrates the difference between human perception and that experienced by other species, however, than the sensory information reported by the pineal gland or "third eye." Though it now appears that we have a functioning pineal gland which may play a part in regulating sexual activity (see Chapter 9), the pineal gland is as important in the second-by-second activities of dozens of vertebrates as ordinary eyes are for man, providing a steady stream of information on a part of the environment humans are simply not conscious of.

The pineal gland is an outgrowth of the brain located, in most species, in the area between the two "ordinary" eyes. Until recently this "third eye" has been little understood and it is still described as "mysterious" even in the textbooks of today. Its strangeness lies in part in the fact that it is the only organ in the brain that is asymmetrical and does not conform to the laws of bilateral symmetry—perhaps because it is one of evolution's oldest organs and may be left over from a time before bilateral symmetry was an operative force. Its strangeness lies also in the contrast between its enormous importance to many species' survival and the fact that it is only very recently that its function has been understood: it is the nonvisual photoreceptor of an independent sensory system not a part of the eyes or any other sense.

In some reptiles, part of the pineal complex called the parietal body is a degenerated third eye that has a lens, a retina with photoreceptors, and several other structures found in a normal eye. Since the parietal eye lacks a set of muscles to move it about, this "third eye" cannot focus on anything or provide any kind of detailed view of the world; indeed, in many species it is covered by a flap of skin or by scales. But the parietal eye *is* sensitive to light. More especially, it now appears that it is sensitive to light at certain angles of polarization; the parietal eye, unlike the ordinary eye, can tell the difference between midday, morning, and evening by responding to the difference between the short, 90-degree polarized light at noon and the longer, off-center angle of the rays at dawn and dusk.

The ability of the parietal eye/pineal gland to detect the position of the sun is, for many species, an essential ingredient of survival. Actually, the position of the sun is used in three different ways by animals such as lizards. On a daily basis, the position of the sun regulates activities needed to keep the animal warm such as basking, perching on branches, or seeking shade to keep it from overheating. Based on the yearly cycle of seasons and the proximity of the sun to the earth, the animal goes through major cycles of reproduction, hibernation, skin color changes, and so forth. And, in a combination of the two, the animal often uses the angle of the sun as a reference signpost to allow it to find home when away from familiar landmarks.

The studies that most clearly show the importance of the parietal eye/pineal gland to animals such as lizards are those in which the organ's access to the outside world is covered with reflective foil or else painted over. Several major changes take place in animals that cannot use their third eyes. For one thing, they tend to spend much more time basking in the sun—as if one of the more important cues to how they regulate their daily behavior had been disturbed. Secondly, animals that are captured, have their third eye blocked, are released, and then are recaptured a year later show marked changes in their reproductive cycles—as if breeding activity had been put on fast-forward. Thirdly, animals temporarily deprived of the third eye and displaced are less able to find their way back to their normal home territories. All three disturbances can be traced to confusion over the position of the sun and probably the angle and polarization of its rays.

The suggestion is not that the parietal eye/pineal gland is the actual clock that governs an animal's activities in relation to the sun. These are a function of internal, biological "clocks" that regulate daily activities (called circadian rhythms because their cycle roughly corresponds to a day in length) and also the longer, circannual rhythms of migration, hibernation, mating, and so forth. Even in total darkness, an animal would still go through sleeping/waking, feeding, grooming, and other daily (circadian) cycles and migration, hibernation, and breeding activities on a yearly (circannual) basis. But the cycles would only be almost (circa) a day or a year in length. It is the pineal gland that synchronizes the internal rhythms with those in the external environment so that the animal's activities correspond with the actual cycles of the sun and nature. That is why animals deprived of the use of their pineal have reproductive cycles that run amok and spend so much time basking in the sun; running on unsynchronized circadian and circannual internal clocks, they are out-of-phase with nature.

The actual mechanism by which such regulation and synchronization takes place has been one of the major findings of science in this area in recent years. To regulate body activities, the pineal gland produces a hormone, melatonin, that is synthesized out of serotonin (the same neural transmitter that is involved in the body's internal pain-killing mechanism). The conversion of serotonin into melatonin depends, in turn, on the production in the pineal gland of the enzyme N-acetyltransferase. And this is the key to the whole interface between circadian rhythms and the rhythms of the sun. For although the production of the enzyme in the pineal (and the resulting serotonin-to-melatonin conversion) follows a roughly circadian rhythm, it is strongly inhibited by the presence of light and stimulated by darkness. Therefore, when it is light, the enzyme is not produced and serotonin is not transformed into melatonin; and when it is dark, melatonin production is increased.

Once secreted by the pineal gland, melatonin plays a major role in regulating sexual activity, principally by inhibiting activity in the gonads (sex organs). During periods of low illumination—such as during the winter, when it would not be appropriate for the animal to come into estrus—the production of the pineal enzyme N-acetyltransferase is increased, increasing the production of pineal melatonin, and thereby slowing down gonadal activity. As the days get longer and illumination increases, the enzyme production and therefore melatonin production is inhibited, and gonadal activity increases.

This link to sex organ activity may also be the mechanism by which the pineal gland regulates such activities as migration. Fluctuations in the activity of the gonads increase and decrease their production of the hormone testosterone, a major factor in migratory behavior. Since testosterone production is regulated by gonadal activity which in turn is regulated by pineal melatonin produced in response to seasonal fluctuations in light levels, this may be one mechanism by which birds are able to know when to begin their migrations.

In the above discussion we have been referring to "the sun" and "illumination" as if they were the same as the angle and polarization of the light. But it must be stressed again that the pineal in some species is sensitive not only to the sun itself and the length of the days as measured by the amount of light, but to the angle and polarization of the sun's rays falling on it.

The most dramatic demonstration thus far of the pineal gland's role in homing has come from the tuna fish, whose pineal gland is able to sense the external environment through a small cartilaginous window in the middle of its forehead. Because of the angle of the window, it is thought that the tuna can actively sense the angle and polarization of the sun's rays, which would reach their maximum intensity in the pineal gland when the sun was 45 to 60 degrees above the horizon. The tuna may be using this information about the angle of the sun as a prime means of navigation.

The significance of all these findings is the fact that humans, too, have intact pineal glands that have been proved to be fully functional, although what exactly they do is not yet fully explained. But if the parallel between human and animal that we have noted throughout this discussion holds true here, the concept is awesome. In the springtime our thoughts turn to dalliance. This could be due, of course, to the balmy weather. But is it not equally possible that we are responding to our pineal gland's perception of the change in light that signifies that we, too, are coming into our breeding season? Are there, then, large-scale hormonal changes in the human species, perhaps linked to sex gland activity, which are in turn regulated by the pineal gland just as migratory behavior is regulated in birds?

If so, what fate is in store for those whose pineals never see the light of day—night workers who are awake in artificial illumination and sleep while the sun is out? The body will eventually adjust to the new schedule, especially if the conversion from daytime to nighttime schedules is done slowly, changing only an hour a week. But can a body that cannot be synchronized with the natural cycles of day and night ever be as happy as one that rises with the sun and sleeps with the moon?

Chapter Four
Tabula Rasa:
The Development of the Human Sensory Systems

When I was a child, I spoke as a child, I understood as a child, I thought as a child; but when I became a man, I put away childish things. For now we see through a glass, darkly, whereas then we will see face to face. Now I know in part, but then shall I know even as also I am known.

I Corinthians 13

From the vast repertoire of sensory abilities outlined in the preceding chapter, the forces of evolution have endowed the human species with those it needs to survive. Since we are not nocturnal, infrared sensing is not important but color vision is. Since we do not fly, echolocation and sonar are not necessary, but broad-spectrum hearing is. Human skin is sensitive to thermal changes so that the body's self-regulating heat mechanisms have a "thermostat." And nociceptive systems warn of the danger points of excess heat, cold, pressure, and so forth.

It comes as somewhat of a surprise, therefore, to learn of a large group of humans who have a very different set of sensory systems. They are not deformed or disabled, nor are they psychics with unusual powers of ESP. Rather, they are human infants.

Again, evolution has been at work. Throughout its nine months in the womb, the infant has gone through a development process that recreates the evolution of the human species—from the days of life in the water as fishes and amphibians, through the early mammalian stages, up to the present status of the species. Thus, the early fetus develops gills and a tail, which disappear in later stages.

This recreation of evolutionary development is also true of the sensory systems. When it is born, the infant's senses are still in the process of transformation from an earlier stage of human development—a time when a somewhat different set of senses was required.

Vision, the dominant sensory system in the human adult, is the last of the sensory systems to develop in the fetus. On the other hand, the ability to detect food odors and other chemical signals, vital to many species' survival, is one of the first systems to develop in the human infant. Thus, the newborn human may actually represent an earlier stage of what the species as a whole went through during the history of its development, a time when vision was not so important, perhaps, but when odors of all kinds played a far greater role.

Physiologically, this early dominance of the olfactory sense may be related to its location in the "reptilian" portion of the brain, a part that has been inherited almost intact from the evolutionary time we spent as reptiles. Children, perhaps representing the earlier stage, may be more sensitive to odors than adults, for whom other sensory experiences somehow mask the older, more primitive sense of smell.

Whether the fetus actually smells anything when surrounded by amniotic fluid is, of course, difficult to assess. But within hours after birth, once the fetal mucus is cleared from the newborn's nose, smells can be discriminated. An infant barely a few hours old can detect unpleasant odors, and will turn away from them—indicating not only that the smell has been received, but that the part of the brain that compares information from the two nostrils is also already functional.

That the sense of smell is working at this early age is quite remarkable, considering its complexity. The receptors, of course, are located inside the nose, embedded in a layer of mucus. Extending into the nasal cavity from the cells are microscopic hairs called cilia on which are located protein particles that act as binding sites for the molecules of odor. When air is directed up into the nose, molecules of odors are attracted to and held by a particular binder site whose chemical composition forms a temporary bond with the particular molecule. This bond changes the cell's ability to pass sodium and phosphorus through the cell wall, which is then translated to the electrical spike of the nervous system.

It was once thought that individual cilia were each receptive to a different kind of molecule, based on their widely differing shapes, and would emit an electrical spike only when that particular molecule landed on the binder site. Like the similar theory advanced about the skin receptors, however, it has since been shown that the shape has nothing to do with the cilia's function (the cells are constantly being replaced, much to the relief of those who snort cocaine, and their shape is a function of the many different stages of growth and decay) and that the cilia can each bind and respond to several different kinds of molecules. This means that a coding scheme is probably at work here as it is in the other sensory systems such as taste. If one receptor is sensitive to molecules A, B, and C, while another is responsive to B, D, and E, then only when the two fire together will the message "molecule B is present" be transmitted. This also helps explain how one smell can modify another (as when perfumes are blended), impossible to account for in the model in which each cilium responds to only one sensation. Molecules from the first odor may still be occupying some of the binding sites involved in the reception of the second odor, diminishing their capacity to report on the second set of molecules. Or the addition of one set of molecules to another may lead the brain to add the two sets of codes together to produce a smell different from either of the originals.

Taste, another of the chemical senses, also functions at an extremely early age. Again, it is unlikely that the fetus does much actual tasting during gestation, but babies are born with a preference for sweet tastes and can sense sourness, bitterness, and saltiness. The sensitivity to salt and bitterness increases as the child grows older.

Newborns can also distinguish among the various kinds of sugars —lactose (milk sugar), fructose (fruit sugar), glucose (simple sugar), and so on. Children retain their preference for sweet substances throughout adolescence, after which the liking for highly sweet foods usually diminishes. This leads to the speculation that the human organism has evolved a liking for sweets based at least partially on their being a highly concentrated source of calories, which are not needed as much in later life.

Teenagers also apparently like salty foods in addition to sweets, the preference for which is acquired some time after an infant is born. The liking for bitter tastes, truly an adult experience, does not appear until even later.

Taste buds begin forming in the fetus during the third month after conception, located in tiny protrusions not only on the tongue but also on the roof of the mouth, on the tonsils, and even down the throat. Some of the protrusions, shaped like thin threads, have no actual role in tasting per se. Others, some shaped like tiny mushrooms which can be seen as small red spots on the tongue, some in the shape of pits, and still others in a leaflike shape, contain one or more of the actual taste bud receptor cells that provide the sense of taste. By later life, the number of taste buds diminishes radically, down to between one or two thousand (a quarter of their number at birth). This means, of course, that it takes considerably more of a substance to produce the same taste sensation. To younger people, therefore, adults seem to oversalt whereas the same food tastes perfectly normal to adult mouths with fewer taste buds.

As discussed in Chapter 1, there is some controversy about whether the various taste sensations (sweet, salty, bitter, and sour) are actually separate tastes or whether they are part of a single taste spectrum. We do know, however, that taste buds themselves are sensitive to different kinds of sensations. Some, those found toward the tip of the tongue, are most sensitive to sweet tastes. Those found in the leaflike protrusions along the edges of the tongue are most sensitive to sour tastes. Salt-sensitive taste buds are found in the mushroom-like protrusions scattered across the surface of the tongue. And bitter tasting is apparently done mainly in the pitlike structures near the back of the tongue. Thus, it can be said that the tongue is most sensitive to sweet at the tip, bitter at the back, and sour at the sides. Salt sensitivity is widespread but somewhat greater at the tip.

Again, the process by which tasting is accomplished is enormously complex, and probably not unlike the odor sensing process described above (although the actual mechanism is still a mystery to scientists). Probably a molecule of the substance in the mouth adheres to a protein binding site on the taste bud, causing changes in the chemistry of the cell that eventually lead to the electrical spike that signals reception.

Smell (and perhaps another sensory system, the vomeronasal system) is important to the infant in a social sense as well—in a baby's ability to detect pheromones, chemical signals given off by others of the same species that communicate various messages such as fear, territorial marking, identification, and so forth. Within two weeks of birth, sleeping children will turn instinctively toward the breast pads of their own mother or a strange mother—food, any food, is essential. But as the infant matures, it becomes more discriminating. At six weeks, the sleeping infant shows a strong preference for its own mother's breast pads rather than those of another woman.

It is probably the same kind of pheromones that enable infants to "mark" their own clothes and blankets so they are clearly identifiable as theirs. The "security blanket" is thus a real phenomenon by which the infant marks and recognizes its own environment by its scent signals—allowing the environment to be transported away from home by taking the blanket along.

The bonding between mother and infant based on scent signals extends both ways. Within forty-eight hours after birth, over half of mothers can identify their infant's bassinet from another's by scent alone—and many can do this within just six hours. This mirrors the observation that pheromones are vital in the mother/child link in many species. In some marsupial animals, for instance, glands in the mother's pouch are used to attract the infant as it makes its long, blind climb to the protective flap of skin. Many mammals, too, use odors to distinguish between their own young and those of other mothers (which they strongly reject).

The status of our sensory systems at birth is far more than simply a by-product of evolutionary development, however. In many ways, the infant is like a different species from the adult it will eventually become, a creature with a very specialized, very different set of needs and a somewhat different set of sensory abilities to fulfill them. A sense of pain, for example, would actually be a detriment to the baby as it is being born, and indeed an infant is insensitive to pain for at least several hours after birth, making the entire process of entry into the world a lot less traumatic than many suppose. (An infant cries in response to the doctor's slap more out of shock than actual pain.) Once the infant does become sensitized, however, the same differences exist in pain response as in later life, and even at an early age there are differences from individual to individual in terms of pain sensitivity.

Skin receptors for heat and cold sensing, on the other hand, are fully functional at birth, allowing the infant to tell the difference between the two (though it has a little more sensitivity for the former than the latter).

As for hearing, it, too, is fairly well developed at birth. An infant not more than two minutes old will correctly turn in the direction of a sound. This indicates, of course, that the hearing mechanism itself is working. But it also proves that the part of the brain that interprets differences between signals from the two ears as a clue to the location of the sound is also functioning or else the baby would not be able to turn in the right direction.

Babies who are blind from birth sometimes develop the even more impressive ability to echolocate. Like a bat, the blind infant will sometimes emit sounds itself which then bounce off the object and reflect back—much like sonar. One baby was observed to make clicking sounds with its tongue and lips that enabled it to detect the presence of a large ball that had been moved silently in front of it, and to then face in the direction of the ball once it had been moved.

Amazingly, it appears that all children are born with this ability to echolocate, even though most never actually learn to use it since other cues are available. Wearing a device which emits sound, even sighted children tested in a dark room can detect the presence of an object by using the returning echoes and make the same gestures—including putting up their hands to interpose a barrier between themselves and an approaching object—as in a normally lit environment.

Perhaps the most startling aspect of infant hearing, however, is that babies may be able to hear sounds *while still within the womb.* For although the fetus's ears are blocked by a gelatin-like substance (which usually drains out of the ears and down the throat within the first day of life), sound can be transmitted through the amniotic fluid and the fluid in the ear in the same way that it travels through water.

Some of the sounds are those inside the mother's body—her breathing and heartbeat, her digestive processes, her muscle and joint movements, the sound of her voice resounding internally.

More interesting, however, is the hypothesis that infants in utero can also use their sense of hearing as a contact with the outside world. The first studies that were done on this involved loud noises, which were shown to increase a baby's breathing rate and general body movements, proving that the sound had been detected. About a month before delivery, the baby will respond with a sudden body movement if a loud horn is sounded.

Additional research has shown, however, that it doesn't take a particularly loud sound to penetrate the womb and the amniotic sac. In an experiment with sheep, a researcher embedded a small microphone next to the embryo inside the mother, then monitored the sounds that penetrated the ewe's unshorn belly, thick skin, womb, and sac. Surprisingly, even normal conversations carried on in the sheep's immediate environment were picked up by the microphone and could be understood. Loud conversations and yelling were almost always heard inside. The implication for humans, of course, is that even without being aware of it, parents begin sensitizing children to their own voices even before the child is born. This may help to explain why babies whose fathers-to-be actively speak to them through the mother's belly end up more responsive to their father's voice once they are born.

Though it is sensitive to a fairly broad set of frequencies, the newborn responds with special attention to the frequencies of cooing and soothing sounds which parents who handle children seem to utter instinctively. It is as if the parent instinctively locates and opens a special communication frequency with the baby which acts to calm and pacify it.

The parent also comes very quickly to recognize the baby's own communications. Three different types of baby cries have been identified, each indicating a different kind of distress: hunger, anger, and pain. So while the mother may not be conscious of what the baby is "saying" (most crying appears to sound the same), she instinctively makes the correct response—to the point where the mother's breast produces more milk in response to her baby's cries of hunger.

In contrast to the chemical and mechanical systems, vision, the dominant sensory system of the human species, is rather poorly developed in infants. When the baby is born, it focuses no more than 12 inches in front of its eyes—about as far away as its own hand. (Indeed, as we will discover, touch and vision are inextricably linked in the period right after birth.) Newborns respond to red as a separate color, while they seem to see blue and green as belonging to the same wavelength.

But beyond this primitive visual ability, the human infant might as well be born like many other animal species—blind. The last system to develop embryonically, vision is the least functional when the infant is born. The retinal cells used in vision begin developing within the first month after conception. By the sixth month, a baby's eyes are sufficiently developed to move together and exhibit a reflex response to light, and a newborn infant can follow a slowly moving object and can distinguish shapes and patterns within its first few days of life. But the part of the nervous system devoted to visual information is far from completed at birth. And, in fact, accurate, detailed vision is not really achieved until age seven!

In the earliest stages of a child's development, nonverbal visual cues from the mother as she leans over the infant are essential to their communication. Pupil size, a major component of this nonverbal visual signaling, plays the same role as it does in later life, and the mother communicates interest (wide-open pupils), anger (closed pupils), and so forth.

At the same time, these early childhood experiences lead to interesting speculations about why adults who have light eyes have been shown to be more sensitive to other people's pupil size than those with dark eyes. The speculation is that light-eyed children are more likely to have had two light-eyed parents whose greater pupil-eye contrast enabled the baby to use this cue at an early age; children with dark eyes may have had no light-eyed parent, meaning that pupil size was not nearly as important in their formative years.

Besides the emotions conveyed by pupil size, infants are capable of recognizing three different facial expressions—happiness, sadness, and surprise—and of imitating all three. Interestingly, a similar distinction between left and right hemisphere brain activity that characterizes the fully developed adult brain (the right hemisphere concentrates on more "intuitive" activities such as pattern recognition while the left hemisphere performs more logical, "mathematical" activities) is also present in infants. Some portions of the ten-month-old child's left hemisphere appear to be reserved for processing "positive" emotional information—this as measured by increased electrical activity in the left hemisphere when it is reacting to a happy expression, as opposed to a sad one.

As the infant develops and its visual range extends out beyond the faces leaning over it, so too does the sophistication of its visual communication abilities. Eight-to-twelve-month-old children can tell the difference between infants and adults, males and females, using a highly specific body communication that is far more complex than size alone (they respond to dwarfs as adults). Shown slides and films of male and female adults and children, infants show the most fear for the adult of the opposite sex but the most preference for an infant of the same sex as itself. How does the infant determine sex? When clothes and toys are present, these are used as clues. But when conflicting clothing is used (as when a boy baby is dressed in a girl's clothes), the infant will correctly identify it as a boy. The answer apparently lies in almost unnoticeable differences in body movement; when an infant is filmed in a dark room with lights attached to its joints so that only the pattern of movement is recorded, other infants can identify it as a boy or a girl. The mechanism for the difference is not yet understood, though two explanations—differences in the skeletal construction of boys and girls, and parental reinforcement of "correct" movement patterns—probably work together to bring it about.

All these observations about a child's sensory systems are especially intriguing since they indicate that the child is somehow different from an adult—that its sensory systems portray a world as different from an adult's as a cat's. At the same time, however, the ways in which a child's senses *do* develop as he or she grows into an adult help to provide a focus on one of the most fundamental concerns in modern sensory system research, namely how much sensory ability an infant is born with versus how much it has to learn. The debate is not over sensory systems alone, however, for it also relates to the understanding of human development in general—whether cognition, perception, and intellect are inborn (the "nature" theory) or whether they are learned by an infant which is truly a tabula rasa (clean slate) when it is born, ready to be taught everything it will come to know (the "nurture" theory).

Let us return to the observation that an infant can apparently sense the direction from which a sound or a smell comes, since it will turn away from bad odors and will turn toward the source of a sound. The question is whether this represents an inherent understanding of spatial relationships—where the object is in relation to the body and how far away—or simply an identification of the direction in which the object lies and not yet correlated, in the infant's brain, with the spatial relationship ability that would indicate how far away.

Certainly by the time a child is old enough to crawl, this ability is fully developed—proved in experiments with a "visual cliff" in which a child crawls out onto a checkerboard pattern stretched out from a table. One area of the checkerboard is optically distorted so that the squares appear smaller, creating the illusion of being further away. The tot, perceiving the illusion as true depth, will not crawl out over the "cliff."

But even a week-old baby demonstrates that its brain processes spatial relationship information. A normal reaction to something being moved toward the face in children of this age is well-defined pupil-widening (alarm), movement of the head to try to avoid the object, and putting hands between its face and the threatening form. An experiment was designed in which two cubes were moved toward the infant's face—a large one held farther away and a smaller one held closer, so that the two would be the same size on the retina. But the infant only shows alarm when the closer, smaller object is moved toward it, indicating that it does, indeed, perceive true object size and distance from its eyes.

Babies will also clutch only at objects that are within their possible range of touch. Though they extend their arms in response to seeing distant objects (the adult equivalent of pointing), true clutching occurs only with objects that are actually close enough to clutch—no matter how much an experimenter may attempt to fool the child with different sized objects.

In certain respects, these examples of extremely early, perhaps inborn, perceptual behavior seem to lend credence to the observations of Gestalt psychology that much of perception is organized around certain basic perceptual rules through which reality is filtered to make it useful. One basic Gestalt rule is "common fate," in which lines and contours of an object that start out together and move together are perceived to be part of the same object. Young infants do, indeed, tend to focus their attention on the outer contours of an object (the outside of a ball, for example) and follow the left and right curved surfaces together as they are moved. But when, in an experiment, the ball shape is broken apart after being moved as a whole, the infants become quite disturbed. So this rule, at least, may be inborn since it is present at such an early age.

The same is true of the Gestalt theory of "good continuation." Because the brain has a preference for particular types of organization, it tends to fill in gaps. So when there are breaks in sequences of still images reaching the retina, as in marquee lights on a movie theater, the brain provides a continuous flow from one arrangement of lights to the next.

On the other hand, not all the Gestalt rules are present in young babies. "Proximity," which explains why an image containing more than two contours will be interpreted as a single object if the contours are closer together than average (the two separate halves of a line drawing of a circle are seen as a single figure rather than two separate contours), does not appear to become functional until the child is at least a year old.

Those who theorize that perceptual responses are learned rather than inborn even point to the early appearance of spatial relationship ability as something that could have been learned in the womb. For although the infant cannot see, it is exposed to a variety of experiences that would help it to define its own body in relation to the surrounding environment.

The debate between innate versus learned behavior is one of considerable antiquity, based on deep philosophical differences that include, among other factors, the debater's particular feelings about the powers of rational thought and free will versus a predetermined fate that has endowed the race with a set of given, inherent powers. Fortunately, however, modern thinking has led to an integration in which both "natural" and "nurtured" have their place.

This thinking is best exemplified by a simple experiment with kittens. Profound changes in adult perception can be caused if, during a critical period of life from three weeks to three months, kittens are kept in a carefully controlled environment in which they are only allowed to see certain patterns. Kittens kept in a white area in which there is no detail fail to develop a normal adult visual sense. Kittens exposed only to a world of vertical patterning develop the ability to see vertical things perfectly normally—furniture legs, for example—but fail to develop the kind of horizontal pattern perception that would allow them to distinguish the edge of a table from which they must jump. Conversely, kittens exposed only to horizontal patterns develop normal vision for horizontal lines but seem to bump into furniture legs as if they didn't exist.

Thus it appears that both developmental processes—learned activity and innate abilities—are involved. The kitten is, indeed, born with an innate ability to learn how to discriminate horizontal and vertical patterns. But unless it comes into contact with features of the environment that somehow "activate" these innate abilities, the innate sense will not develop. Since there are rather distinct neural pathways for horizontal and vertical components of vision, the stimulation of both is required for normal sight.

The implications of this explanation when applied to the human baby are indeed profound. Like kittens, human babies are born with the ability to learn how to use their sensory systems. Much of the development of these systems can only take place, however, in the presence of environmental signals.

One striking example of this process is the ability to recognize sounds. The infant is born with the ability to distinguish some forty consonantal sounds—the noncontinuous sounds of the language produced by the various positions of the lips, tongue, throat, etc. By the time a child is six, however, its ability to perceive consonantal sounds has been severely reduced; exposed to the speech of its parents and others, only the sounds it will need—the particular consonants of its particular language—have been reinforced and retained.

One of the most exciting aspects of this psychological model is that it has a direct counterpart—perhaps even an explanation—in the physiological development of the fetal brain. In the first chapter, we described the importance of the organization of the brain into distinct maps that reflect either the world or the part of the body that senses it—a specific area devoted to the hand and its fingers in the brain cortex that processes touch sensations, for example. The question that has puzzled scientists is how the nerve fibers that grow toward the brain from the hand as the nervous system is developing find their way to the right brain area, and how the actual map is formed.

One theory is that the axons growing from the hand are simply labeled with a chemical compound that has an appropriate receptor compound in the correct part of the brain. But this would require so elaborate a scheme of coding that it seems all but impossible to assume that each and every nerve fiber from each and every sensory system has its own special code. Rather, the latest theory is that the formation of the map areas follows a two-fold process. First, nerve fibers find their way to the correct part of the brain through a general chemical coding scheme that directs chemicals on the nerve fiber to within the general quadrant of the brain where they are to form synapses. This much is innate.

But then a second phase takes over. Only those nerves that are actually stimulated repeatedly form lasting synapses, strengthened by neurochemical processes; the other synapses simply disappear. In other words, experience itself forms the sensory mechanism used for its perception.

In the early, formative stage of development, when the synaptic pathways are being worked out, sensory stimulation from one system can substitute for another in the establishment of perceptual "frameworks" such as spatial relationships. Vision, for instance, is not necessary for the development of depth perception. In fact, as is clear from observing blind and/or deaf children, virtually any sensory input is enough to define the spatial relationship ability— which remains every bit as precise even if the input of one of the sensory systems is denied.

On a more practical level, this new theory of a two-stage developmental process also puts an infant's touch/vision relationship in a whole new light. The classic assumption has been, of course, that the infant's 12-inch visual range, coupled with its continual reaching out to grasp objects in front of it, is the process through which a baby learns to associate the two kinds of sensory input—vision and touch. In this way, it was assumed, what information was provided by the eyes about an object's tactile qualities—its smoothness or roughness, hardness or softness, etc.—and its distance from the body would be borne out by the tactile sense.

In the new model, however, quite the reverse is suggested: an infant, born into a Garden-of-Eden-like existence in which all things appear as one. Thus the infant, at birth, may be essentially synesthetic; that is, one sensory experience can trigger perception by another system, and the infant may see sounds as easily as it hears them. If a baby is shown a "virtual" image—a projected shape that appears real—it will grasp at it and be intensely disappointed that its hands do not make contact because its visual system has predicted with utmost certainty what its tactile system should be experiencing. The same link with the tactile sense is true with hearing. A baby that hears a sound in a darkened room will reach out and try to grab it—even at a very early age. And a baby that sees its mother through a glass but hears her voice over a loud-speaker coming from a different direction will become agitated; its visual sense had predicted where the sound was to come from.

What's more, even blind babies up to a certain age turn their eyes and actually look at a source of sound at the same time they will try to grab it—again an indication that there is a major unity of sensory experience in the newborn.

As the child grows, however, the brain becomes more specialized. Nerves from the eyes that terminate in specific areas of the visual cortex are strengthened, whereas nerves projecting elsewhere begin to atrophy. And so, by six months, the child actually senses less than it did at birth. The brain centers are differentiated; nerves from the eyes terminate only in the visual cortex, and so forth. Children of six months somehow know that vision and hearing and touching are different senses—that one cannot completely predict the input of another. Though they will still grasp at the virtual image, their grasp is different and they are no longer nearly as disturbed. If one covers the face of a six-month-plus child who is grasping an object, he/she will drop it since it can no longer be seen. Only later will the separate coordination skills between the two be learned again.

What this model suggests, in fact, is an entirely new way of thinking about sensory systems, as fundamental as the new thinking about the organization of the brain itself. For it is now starting to be suggested that it is the acquisition of various skills, such as distinguishing among the different sensory systems, that provides the impetus for the brain's division of functions into right and left hemisphere activities. In other words, rather than innate structural differences between right and left hemispheres resulting in a divi-sion of activities, it is the development of the activities themselves that causes the specialization of the two hemispheres.

It is awesome to realize that this model has ramifications far beyond the sensory systems alone, even as important as these are. For the controversy which the new model seeks to mediate— whether development is due to learned behavior or innate abilities —has been perhaps *the* most perplexing scientific question of all time.

Quite simply, the same model used to explain how sensory systems develop can also describe the development of general intellectual thought processes as well. What's more, the connection between the two may lie in their actual interrelationship so that the very nature of human intellect and cognition may depend on how a child's sensory systems develop and are stimulated. The clearest example is Infant Stimulation ("infant stim" in medical jargon), which has shown quite conclusively that stimulating a child visually by presenting it with various unusually patterned toys and mobiles actually increases its general alertness level and responsiveness to other learning situations.

The link between general human intelligence and the sensory systems is much more profound, however, than that both seem to develop through the stimulation of innate tendencies by the environment. Cognition and perception are, in fact, linked through the most basic human activity: language. And some researchers now believe that it is the actual development of language that is responsible for many of the phenomena of perception.

The relationship between language and perception has always been a fruitful area for study, and the ability to visualize something internally is closely linked with the ability to describe it verbally. Verbal and written descriptions create highly specific mental images. The same is true, though to a lesser extent, with sounds, which often evoke vivid mental images of favorite places or scenes. It is as if memory itself were linked to these verbal descriptions and thence to consciousness.

The link between vision, visual memory, and verbalization can be quite startling. Even though the actual vision may have lasted only a few seconds, the passerby who sees a bank robber running off may be able to describe the face with complete accuracy. And what author has ever "seen" the future so vividly portrayed in science fiction stories? What artist has to "see" images in the mind's eye to paint them clearly on canvas?

This process applies to ordinary visual perceptions, too. Imagine, for example, that it is a bright, sunny day and you are standing in the midst of a field of wildflowers. The field is surrounded by a wooden rail fence. On one of the fence posts, a small fly is sitting, its wings glistening in the sun. Suddenly an airplane passes overhead, its shadow falling briefly on the fly. The insect is startled, flies up and over to the next field, and settles on the back of a large brown horse.

The point is that although one may never have actually seen a field of wildflowers on a sunny day, or a brown horse, the brain is able to synthesize the mental picture from the verbal description, and give life to the little story above. As the poet Emily Dickinson writes:

> I never saw a moor,
> I never saw the sea;
> Yet know I how the heather looks,
> And what a wave must be.

This link with verbalization is not present, however, with the sense of smell. Most adults have a strictly limited vocabulary when it comes to odor description, and can remember very few words for smells (unlike, for example, words that describe colors). The vocabulary seems to depend on how strong the smell is or its associations rather than on the aroma itself. It is virtually impossible to describe an odor to someone else who hasn't already experienced it. And smells, except for general groupings such as "sweet" or "nauseating," do not lend themselves to easy categorization, as if each smell were a separate entity unrelated to other smells. This is in spite of attempts to scientifically classify smells into groups—flowery, putrid, fruity, spicy, resinous, and burned, according to one popular scheme. The classification, of course, has nothing whatsoever to do with what, for instance, freshly brewed coffee actually smells like, or how it is similar to or different from hot apple pie.

In a recent study it was shown that people could distinguish very few scents without being given clues as to their nature. However, given the correct vocabulary and having the smells identified for them the first time, the group did extremely well in further identification tests.

There was no study done to see if the verbal labels were remembered after a longer time period had elapsed, but one would suspect that they were not, simply because the sense of smell does not seem to be related to conscious thought processes, which are vital to language. The intriguing explanation is that since the sense of smell develops before language does and is so important in early life, perhaps smells are remembered differently by the brain. Certainly there seems to be no limit on memory length with the memory of smells, so that childhood odor experiences will come flooding back even late in adult life. This has led to the even more fascinating suggestion that déjà vu—the sensation that something has been experienced or seen before—may be a form of olfactory sensory memory. At one time, a smell was perceived and stored away with certain emotionally charged feelings about the place or the time. Subsequently, later in life, the same smell reactivates the hidden-away memories, which come flooding into the mind as an extremely deep, unidentified sensory memory.

Returning to vision and its connection with language, it is evident that not only can language stimulate the mental image, but it can also affect what is actually seen by the eyes. A story is told of a linguist who, while working as an insurance investigator to earn his keep, came across a factory accident in which a worker had tossed his cigarette butt into a supposedly empty oil drum, only to have the vapors in the drum explode and injure him. If the language had a word for "full of vapors," reasoned the linguist, and not simply "empty" or "full," the man might have thought to himself "drum filled with vapors" and not "empty drum" and might have thrown his cigarette elsewhere.

The story suggests, of course, that language may define perception as strongly as perception defines language, the common assumption. This idea has found support in studies of the perceptual abilities of people who speak different languages. For example, because of the constant presence of snow and ice, the Eskimo language has over twenty-nine words to describe the various shades of white (similar to our English pale white, cream, off-white, and so on, but far more numerous). Apparently, Eskimos actually perceive more detail in snow than those of us who simply look at it and think "white." The same thing is true of American Indians living in the desert, who have many more words for red and sand colors than occur in English. Again, the native speaker actually is able to distinguish more in the environment. In the other extreme, certain Australian tribes have only three color responses, one for the colors red, purple, and orange, a second encompassing white, yellow, and green, and the third to designate black, blue and violet.

The issue of significance here, however, is not that there is a connection between linguistic and sensory experiences—that is accepted as commonplace today. Rather, interest among sensory researchers and linguists alike has centered on discovering the exact nature of the link between them. And more and more it appears they are connected from an extremely early age, and obey similar models of development.

Development of visual perception in a kitten, which we mentioned earlier, in which the kitten's ability to see horizontal and vertical patterns must be stimulated by actual exposure to horizontal and vertical patterns in order to develop, is an appropriate analogy to the development of language in humans, according to the leading advocate of this theory, linguist Noam Chomsky. The child, according to Chomsky, is born with a set of innate language learning abilities centered in a small area on the brain's left temporal lobe. Like sensory systems, however, the innate language learning ability must be stimulated at the proper age—at which time the child develops its actual ability to speak and understand its native language.

Testing the hypothesis of stimulated development of an innate ability is virtually impossible, of course, since children cannot be used in experiments in which they are prevented from hearing speech in normal situations. But back in the Middle Ages, Frederick

II, emperor of the Holy Roman Empire, attempted to settle an argument about which language was the most "natural" by separating a group of babies at birth and forbidding anyone to speak with them. He wanted to see what their first words would be if left completely to their own devices—Latin, Greek, Hebrew, or the local language. Unfortunately, all the babies died before they could say anything.

Some proof, however, is afforded by the examples of two "wild" children, one a twelve-year-old boy discovered in France in the 1700s who had evidently survived being abandoned in the woods by his parents at birth (the subject of François Truffaut's film *L'Enfant Sauvage*), the other a thirteen-year-old girl ("Genie") discovered some fifteen years ago whose parents had kept her chained in a room from infancy and had never spoken to her. Both children failed to develop language abilities even after extensive tutoring in later life, indicating that if the child is not exposed to language during a critical period, its ability to develop linguistically will be thwarted just as development of visual perception was thwarted in the kittens who cannot see verticals or horizontals.

For Chomsky, the development of language ability thus follows precisely the same course as the development of sensory systems. And the presence of a language center in a physiologically defined area of the brain means that it develops connections with the surrounding world just as do hearing or sight or touch. In the same way that a child does not have to "learn" how to see, according to Chomsky, so it really does not need to learn language. How else can children with very little exposure to sophisticated language so easily recognize the difference between a grammatical and an ungrammatical sentence, unless it is because their language learning is based on certain "linguistic universals" with which they are born, like hands and feet?

Not all linguists agree with Chomsky, of course. Jean Piaget, for instance, sees language as only one example of a whole range of general intellectual capabilities—a faculty that develops only once these other capabilities have been formulated. The thrust of Piaget's argument is that the intellectual development of the child goes through certain inevitable stages, in specific sequence, and at a relatively invariable rhythm. The stages, curiously enough, mirror the development of intellectual thought throughout history—beginning with concepts of number, then concepts of class, and so forth. According to Piaget, at the age of two, immediately following the emergence of the symbolic capacity, the child exhibits its first manifestation of language. Thus symbolic capacity, greater/lesser and more/less distinctions, notions of time and space, notions of category or class, and so forth, are a basic set of general intellectual abilities which then develop into language and representation.

This brief digression into the field of linguistics has been necessary because it is at the very essence of the link between language and the senses. Putting two and two together to get five, scientists have begun reasoning that it may be the acquisition of language itself that results in the differentiation of left and right hemispheres and that language itself therefore has a profound effect on the experience of sensory phenomena.

The link between activity in the two brain hemispheres and the general field of perception and cognition has already been noted as one of the major "eye-openers" of modern psychological and physiological investigation. The left hemisphere, tied to the right side of the body, contains much of the brain's processing information for logic, numbers, language, and rational thought. The right hemisphere, tied to the left side of the body, appears to be far more concerned with pattern recognition, color perception, shape discrimination, and so forth—the more aesthetic, artistic side of the species.

Susan Curtiss, one of the researchers who worked with "Genie," noticed that the wild girl seemed to rely on her right hemisphere almost exclusively. Tests in which she was asked to identify two sounds that were presented to left and right ears simultaneously showed that she invariably "listened" more to her left ear. More important, she performed tasks that normally are centered in the right hemisphere—such as facial feature recognition—extremely well, while her linguistic skills (normally a left hemisphere function) were those of an extremely young child. Again, tests showed that she also used her right hemisphere for sentence recognition, and her limited vocabulary indicated a reliance on right hemisphere activity as well—she spoke of the size and color of objects, rather than their movement or relations ("red ball" rather than "throw ball"), again indicating she was operating with the more visual, right hemisphere even when it came to language.

These observations led Curtiss to suggest that it is the development of language itself that causes the brain to split its functions between left and right hemisphere activities, and that the absence of proper stimulation of the language center in the left hemisphere may profoundly affect the whole organization of the brain. This has also been borne out by studies on deaf children who are not taught sign language in infancy; they fail to develop the various left and right hemisphere specializations found in normal children. Deaf infants who are taught sign language, on the other hand, develop a normal differentiation between left and right hemisphere activities, with the language center in the left hemisphere developing quite normally.

The significant finding in this latter group of children who are taught sign language, however, is that their picture-recognizing abilities, normally a function of the right hemisphere, have now become part of the left hemisphere's activities. In other words, the development of language skills has rearranged the brain to correspond with the language/picture recognizing ability required in signing. Something similar might occur with blind children taught in infancy to determine positions and features by means of electronic echolocators equipped with receivers in both ears. Since auditory memory seems to center in the left hemisphere, it is possible that these children would center their memory of spatial relationships there too, even though the perception of spatial relationships is usually a function of the right hemisphere.

The implication in all these observations, of course, is that the very structure of the brain itself is somehow influenced by actual experiences of the world. It is a new and obviously radical departure from classic explanations that suggest either that the senses and nature are in harmony so that we perceive the true nature of the universe, or else that the human organism, complete with its rather inadequate sensory systems, is plunked down into a hostile environment to which it must adapt to survive. The new model suggests, on the other hand, that the environment itself is partially responsible for determining which sensory systems will be important to the species, and which pathways within those systems will be reinforced and survive.

Chapter Five
The Human Semaphore:
The Languages of Nonverbal Sensory Communication

See me, feel me, touch me, heal me . . .

The Who, TOMMY

What do you remember of the last person you saw? Male or female? Hair length and color? Clothing? Perfume? Eye, skin color? Height? Voice qualities? Mannerisms? "Intelligence"? A certain something that attracted you?

How do you describe the person who excites you? A fifth-century Irish manuscript contains this glowing description of Etain, the fairest maiden in the land:

> A tunic she wore with a long hood that covered her head. It was made of green silk, with gold and red embroidery, clasped over her breasts with beautiful silver clasps; . . . bright gold and the green flashing in the sun.
>
> Each of her arms was as white as new-fallen snow and each of her cheeks was as red as foxglove. Even and small were the teeth in her head, and they shone like pearls. Her eyes were as blue as hyacinth, her lips delicate and crimson. Very high, soft and white were her

shoulders. Her knees were round and firm and white, her ankles as straight as a carpenter's rule. Her feet were slim and as white as the ocean's foam. Her eyes were evenly set and her eyebrows a bluish-black color like a beetle.

The senses in action, at their peak. Not being used to sniff out food or warn the individual of danger, they have turned to a perhaps even more important activity: intraspecies communication—specifically, sexual communication. Survival of the species depends on successful mating, mating depends on an eligible partner, and finding a partner depends on a sensory system capable of detecting the messages given off by other members of the species—both those that invite the courtship ritual and those that warn "Stay away, not interested," or, even more threatening, "Stay away, this one is mine!"

Humans, like most other species, are constantly both giving off and receiving massive amounts of sensory information about each other—sexual preferences and willingness to copulate (chemical secretions, perfumes, clothing styles); whether we're aggressive individuals ready to fight (fist shaking, the tightened lips/wrinkled forehead display meant to terrorize) or more passive types who would probably rather avoid a skirmish (bodily withdrawal, head bowing); where and when we last ate (chemical signals); how much we are participants in a particular subgroup within the society (jargon, mannerisms) or how rebellious we are (clothing, hair styles, body adornments); and so forth.

Much has been made of the parallels between the human and other animal species when it comes to these sensory signals indicating sexuality, aggression, territorial marking, and so forth. And indeed, there is not a lot of difference between the animal that marks its territory by laying down scents in its urine and dung and the human activity of marking home boundaries with lawn ornaments and door decorations. Or between the animal that adopts various defensive postures when threatened, then finally strikes back, and the human animal when it is attacked.

The same similarity holds true for parallels between the elaborate courtship displays found throughout the animal world (birds flashing bright plumage, to name but one example) and those of the human world (adolescent clothing styles, for example). To be picked as a mate, you've got to be noticed.

But what makes *human* communication unique, of course, is that we often have a choice over what information we provide to another's sensory systems—a conscious manipulation of visual, auditory, and chemical information in which the words of spoken languages are just the beginning.

There is, of course, a big difference between conscious and unconscious, overt and hidden forms of communication. Those who are masters of sensory manipulation—including everyone from Madison Avenue advertising executives to sleight-of-hand artists—usually owe their success to an ability to consciously juggle the unconscious signals. Knowing, for instance, that in contemporary Western culture crossed legs indicate a barrier whereas open legs signify an invitation to come over, television ads for pleasure products invariably show people with their legs open.

But manipulation of conscious, everyday signals can be every bit as meaningful and potent. In even the most routine social interactions, the semaphore (from the Greek words signifying "meaning-bearing") is clicking away its messages to whoever wants to attend to them. Choosing to wear a red dress is a signal ("Notice me!"). Not choosing to wear a suit and tie to work is a signal ("I'm different"). Designer jeans are a signal ("I belong to a certain peer group"). Talking with a dialect is a signal ("I'm part of a certain geographical region and economic group"). And so on. Virtually every decision that is made from getting dressed in the morning to going to bed is some kind of signal to someone. Only in sleep is the semaphore system really quiet.

Every part of the body is involved. Since the first visual contact made with others is generally with the face and head, hair is of vital importance. It immediately identifies male or female, while giving plenty of opportunity for individual expression of the person's relationship to (or lack of concern for) peers and the general cultural values.

Clothing comes next, with the culture again determining what is beautiful or unusual or daring, and whether the individual conforms to or differs from the society's values. This is also true for lack of clothing and the exposure of various parts of the female body, from breasts to legs. For the Victorians, merely uncovering the ankles was considered immodest; in Western culture of today, the mini-skirt is making a comeback. Uncovering breasts in public in Western culture is still considered highly offensive, although in many other countries the breast is no more a sexual object to be covered up than the foot is in America.

Not all of the nonverbal signals of body language are concerned with external choices, of course. All by itself the body is enormously communicative. Different ways women fold their arms across their chests can be explained as inviting or discouraging another's approach, depending on whether the breasts are covered. Other signals, too, indicate whether a person is or isn't "available" and open to being approached.

Probably left over from the time before humans developed symbolic spoken language and relied on grunts and gestures instead, the body can also articulate quite a range of feelings. Using facial expressions alone as a visual cue, persons from many different cultures are able to recognize some six basic emotional states: happiness, surprise, fear, sadness, anger, and disgust.

To these "basic" emotions communicated visually by facial expressions can be added some 130 other nonvocal physical gestures, postures, and so forth, and some two dozen distinct nonverbal grunts, whistles, moans, shrieks, and the like, all communicating over 20 basic types of messages. In fact, it's thought that some 93 percent of all the information that is conveyed in a typical utterance is conveyed by nonverbal and nonvocal signs—vocal inflections, body gestures, tongue cluckings, and so on.

In every sense of the word, this kind of communication is a true language—with individual elements that can be understood separately (the symbolic meaning of a red dress, for instance) and also placed together into meaningful patterns (an evaluation of a person's total physical demeanor, hair style, perfume, etc.) Like spoken language, all these conscious means of communication are learned. And just as there are no inherent properties of any of the sounds of a spoken language (there is nothing in the word *hat* that actually suggests the shape or function of the object it represents), so the relationships between the elements of visual communication and their meanings is purely arbitrary. There is nothing inherent in the color red to associate it with danger or excitement; the relationship is as arbitrary as the use of tattoos and lip-stretching in some cultures to provoke sexual interest, a practice completely alien to our culture.

These signs and signals of the visual language of the body all obviously take advantage of the fact that, for most humans, "seeing is believing." Despite the importance of the other senses to survival (try and imagine what it would be like not to *feel* anything), humans tend to trust information conveyed by the eyes above data provided by any of the other senses. We insist that we "see" water in a desert mirage even though the brain tells us this can't possibly be so. And we give credence to "ghosts" and "apparitions" even though all the other senses report that there's nothing there.

Much of the understanding of what goes on in the visual signaling process stems, of course, from the physiological processes involved in vision itself. Real knowledge of the process only began as recently as the early 1960s, when it was discovered that the two types of cells found in the light-sensing portion of the retina—rod-shaped cells ("rods") located around the periphery of the retina and cone-shaped cells ("cones") located at the center (the fovea)—are actually part of two somewhat separate visual sensory systems.

The system connected to the at least 120 million rods in each eye takes in information on 500 levels of lightness and darkness in the environment to form images of contours and patterns—a black-and-white image of how much light objects and their background reflect. The other, connected to the 7 million cones in each eye, both contributes to the perception of forms and also gives humans a unique color vision ability capable of distinguishing some one million combinations of color hue, saturation, and brightness.

The rod and cone cells in the retina are basically similar to virtually every other type of nerve receptor. Specialized transducers, they convert one form of physical energy into another, in this case the electromagnetic energy of visible light—ranging from the color violet at a wavelength of around 400 nanometers * to the color red at around 700 nanometers—into the bioelectrical energy of nerve impulses.

This is accomplished by light-sensing chemicals which absorb the photon energy present in light waves, are momentarily transformed into another chemical substance by the addition of the energy, and then re-release the energy in the form of a small electrical spike in a nerve as the chemical returns to its original state. Chemicals in the thin, elongated rods are sensitive to all the wavelengths of visible light, and are therefore capable of distinguishing only degrees of intensity. The chemicals in the three types of shorter, squatter cones, on the other hand, absorb only one particular wavelength (color) of visible light, and emit electrical spikes only when hit by that wavelength. In the same way that paint colors can be analyzed into different combinations of the primary colors, so the red-, green-, and blue-sensing cones analyze light based on its proportions of the three basic colors.

As in the process of pain response described earlier, however, the real work of visual perception takes place as a result of higher-order information processing in the brain. Since each cell in the retina can only respond as "on" or "off" when stimulated by light, higher levels of the nervous system must act to interpret the information and organize it into patterns. This is accomplished by having the various cells of the retina feed into more and more complex nerve cells as the electrical signals travel toward the brain, so that eventually there are small groups of cells receiving information originally sensed by many thousands of retinal cells. The many cells which feed into a complex cell comprise its receptive field.

This process culminates in the cerebral cortex, the layer of "gray matter" covering the rest of the human brain where most of the more sophisticated types of neural activity take place. The cortex

---

* A nanometer equals one billionth of a meter.

comprises some 45 square centimeters of the brain and contains some 100,000 cells per square millimeter—a truly massive nerve center, more highly developed in man than in any other species. The cortex is divided into specialized areas of brain activity (a language center, a hearing center, and so forth), and several areas are devoted to the various aspects of vision (the frontal area controls the movement of the eyes, for example). But it is the striate or visual cortex where most of the activity surrounding actual "seeing" takes place.

The visual cortex in the brain is spatially organized to correspond to very specific parts of what is being seen (the visual field). The neurons are arranged so that the brain maintains a "map" of up and down, left, right, and center locations that correspond to where the image originated (light entering the eye from the left of the field of vision is focused by the lens on an area at the right of the retina, which then sends its information back to an area in the right hemisphere of the cortex that corresponds to the left side of the visual field). There is also almost total separation between the vision of the right eye and the vision of the left eye until the very final stage of the visual process, since the cortex is organized into side-by-side bands of nerve layers devoted to either right-eye or left-eye perception. And more sensitive portions of the retina correspond to more detailed sections of the "map" (in the case of the center of the eye, the receptive fields are quite close together, and each processes information from only approximately 4 degrees of the visual field— the area covered by the fingers when held at arm's length).

What makes the visual system so unique and allows such precise discrimination among forms is that many different nerves, each sensitive to a particular kind of stimulation, are trained on any given area of the visual field. Thus, for example, while some cells process information created by a spot of light, others analyze the information generated by a moving line in the same visual area.

It is as if, at a corporate meeting (an area on the retina), representatives from each department (cells forming different receptive fields) were given the same information (light from a particular area of the visual field), then carried it back to the department (cells in the central nervous system) where it could be acted on. Thus, there might be eight or nine receptive fields working on different features of essentially the same piece of visual information.

Continuing this analogy of the corporate meeting, it is as if each department head (higher-order cell) sent several representatives (rod cells comprising the receptive field), but would only act on the information if the right combination of representatives reported favorably. For example, many receptive fields of these higher-order cells are organized concentrically. When input from the center of the field activates the higher-order neuron, stimulation from the outer edge of the field inhibits it. Thus a small spot which activates only the center cells of a receptive field is a strong stimulus, while a larger one, which spills over into the inhibitory periphery, generates a weaker impulse. This is the reason why a small, focused light is easier to see than a larger, diffuse one.

Other integrating cells are particularly sensitive to lines at various slants so that they provide their maximum output when a line crosses the cells in its receptive field within a narrowly defined angle of 19 to 20 degrees. For example, if the corner of a picture frame is in the upper right portion of the field of view, the angle will fall across rod cells which send impulses to many higher-order cells; but only the cells sensitive to horizontal and vertical lines (the elements of the right angle) will be stimulated to fire when their rod cells are exposed to this pattern; those sensitive to diagonal lines will remain inactive.

Other integrating cells called moving bar detectors are sensitive only to lines which move through them at particular angles, so that as the eye sweeps over a form only those receptors attuned to that angle are stimulated to respond.

And all of the analyzing cells mentioned above also have completely opposite counterparts—for example, bar detectors which respond strongly when a light line silhouetted by a dark background crosses the visual field at the receptive field's angle.

In the final stage of visual perception, information from all the various receptive fields is integrated into brain cell patterns which correspond in a distorted but systematic way with the image that first entered the eye. Again our analogy with the large corporation is appropriate. Just as each department has a hierarchy in which one level reports more and more complex information to the next, so the various brain cells that form the receptive fields, from the simple on/off variety to the complex moving bar detector type, are arranged in layers of increasing sophistication; the output of one kind feeds directly into the next type. But just as the corporate department works internally until the very highest stage of the hierarchy, so the information from the different receptive fields is also kept discrete as it passes from one level of complexity to the next. Thus, the brain maintains the almost complete autonomy of the different elements of the visual field in the same way that right- and left-eye perception are kept separated; pattern information (such as the right angle in our picture frame example) from the upper left part of the visual field is kept together with other information from that part of the visual field almost intact as it passes from one level of brain processing to the next. It is only at the very last stage that the brain can "see" the right angle of the picture frame, place it in the upper left part of the visual field, and interpret information from one eye as slightly different from the other (thereby enabling depth perception). In the corporate analogy, the brain is the company president who acts only on the advice of his VPs.

As for color vision, it too is organized into receptive fields, but they are completely separate from those used for pattern perception until the very last stage of the brain's interpretive process.

Information from all three types of cone cells (red-, green-, and blue-sensitive) must be present for normal color vision to take place, and the brain apparently needs continual sources of color contrast to keep active or else it simply adapts to the color and stops reporting its perception (as we have also seen to be the case with adaptations to taste, smell, and other sensory experiences). In a situation in which only one set of receptors is stimulated, color vision is impossible—as is the case in "graying out," in which airplane pilots flying through blue, cloudless skies report a temporary loss of *all* color vision.

Like the rods, the cones transmit messages to cells in the visual cortex which organize them into meaningful patterns. In the case of color vision, however, the receptive fields are based on sensitivity to one of the three primary colors rather than the bar and pattern detectors of the rod-based fields. For example, one type of color neuron found in the retina and at higher levels receives input from two different types of cones—those sensitive to red and those sensitive to green. Some of these neurons are excited when they receive stimulation from red cone cells and inhibited by stimulation from green-sensing cones; for other neurons, the exact reverse is true. Thus, red and green are analyzed by a code-like stimulated/inhibited pattern of nerve impulses not unlike that found in the rod system. This is why staring intently at a red square will produce a green afterimage square when one looks away. The red-sensing cones have been overstimulated, and without their input the cells they inhibit are free to send a "clean" message to the brain. This relationship between green and red sensing is why these colors are so often "opposed" to one another in sign systems of various sorts (traffic lights, for example).

Blue/yellow sensing is a somewhat separate and more complicated color sensing apparatus. Higher-level neurons in this system receive input from a receptive field in which red- and green-sensing cones surround blue-sensing cones, or the reverse—an arrangement that allows the neuron to respond to several different colors. These neurons are excited by stimulation from blue receptors and inhibited by red/green cone stimulation. Blue light is most effective in activating and yellow light best inhibits them. Again, the yellow afterimage produced by staring at a blue shape is a clear illustration of the process.

The net result of these processes is a visual system that is extremely sensitive to a rather limited portion of the electromagnetic spectrum, even within the part defined as visible light. The greatest cone cell sensitivity is to blue light at around 400 nanometers, followed by green, and then red, with a fairly extensive gap between green and blue. Overall, however, the eye's greatest sensitivity is to green, partially because the rods are more sensitive to bluish-green light, especially at low light levels (reds and oranges are the first colors to disappear at night).

Simultaneously with all this activity in the visual cortex, several other brain centers are active in the process of perception. Pupil size (the response to how bright an object is) and focus (the response to the distance of the object from the eye) are controlled completely independently of the actual content of visual information processed in the visual cortex. Those with brain damage to the cortex that prevents vision can still exhibit an uncanny ability to accurately direct their eyes toward a source of light even though they report seeing absolutely nothing.

The physiological process that directs attention to features of the environment which we want to focus on is designed to direct the eye to place the object of interest in the center of the field of view where the retina is so much more sensitive than on the periphery.

The process begins as the eye is moved about in seemingly random scans, known as saccades, across an object. After each scan, the eye stops, spending some 50 milliseconds to analyze what the fovea (central part of the retina) is focused on. (Saccades are apparently directed by the frontal lobe, a separate part of the cerebral cortex. They operate even when the individual is asleep and the visual cortex is receiving no stimulation, when they are known as REM, or rapid eye movements. Saccades also direct vision while reading, allowing the eye to jump from one group of words to the next.)

Once an object or feature seen by the fovea becomes "worth paying attention to," however, saccade activity changes and a different part of the brain takes over. A very definite pattern of eye scans emerges in which the brain directs the center of gaze to quickly take account of whatever has attracted attention.

The most interesting studies of this rapid scanning activity in humans have been responses to advertising messages—how experimental subjects react, for example, to a new package design, and specifically where the eye falls when looking at advertisements. In Michael Crichton's film *Looker,* this was carried to the extreme, and an ad agency of the not-too-distant future used highly accurate eye movement tracings to create the perfect, computer-simulated ads in which the viewer's eye would fall precisely where the agency wanted. Current agencies haven't yet achieved this level of sophistication. But laboratory research on animal saccades (including chimpanzee eye movements) is becoming more and more precise so that, with chimps at least, researchers can tell exactly what features of another chimp's face attract the most attention.

Eye movement tracings are particularly interesting when linked with images of potential sexual arousal. Human eyes move very quickly to scan the face, then progress almost immediately to the chest, then the genital area, then back to the face. When looking at the face itself, the eyes are the first area most intently studied, followed by quick excursions down to the mouth, stopping by the nose on the way back to the eyes.

In addition to eye movement, the rest of the neurophysiology of visual attention is also just beginning to be understood. Separate from the saccade mechanism, another area of the cortex, called the posterior parietal cortex, acts on the same neural information provided to the visual cortex; the nerves running back to the brain from the eye actually split into two separate pathways, one to the visual cortex, where the information is processed as visual information in the process described above, the other to the posterior parietal cortex, where the same information is processed in the "attention paying" center.

Under normal circumstances, when one is alert but not paying attention to anything in particular, the posterior parietal cortex receives and processes information from the retina in a normal, unexcited way. But if something in the environment is "different" —a flash of light, for example, or an object of a different color than the background—the cells of the posterior parietal cortex begin to fire more actively. This, in turn, causes a signal to be transmitted to the frontal lobe, which directs a saccade toward the object of interest, putting it in the center of the field of view. With the eye thus concentrating on something, and with increased nerve activity of both the posterior parietal cortex and the frontal lobe, the cells in the visual cortex also become stimulated to pay attention to the incoming data from the retina and analyze the subject of vision. Thus, all three areas of the brain devoted to vision are called into play when we are attending to something special in the visual environment.

Paying attention to something thus has the immediate physiological effect of putting more of the brain's perceptive processes to work studying the object. Without this mechanism—a condition of those with damage to the posterior parietal cortex as happens following a stroke—a person can *see* objects but cannot pay attention to them; if the damage is only to one side of the brain—the right, for example—the person will find it virtually impossible to notice or, therefore, remember things happening on the left side of the field of view.

And yet, despite all that is coming to be known of the neurological and physiological processes of vision, the ultimate question— how, actually, do we see, how is all the information integrated—is still somewhat of a mystery. For the final integration of visual data into images is apparently a function of still uncertain psychological processes in which the data representing what is seen by the eyes is somehow compared with and coordinated by internal representations stored in memory. These enable the neurological output of the visual cortex to be converted into something more meaningful to the organism.

One example is the almost computer-like "program" that automatically assigns a top, bottom, and sides to an object when it is first perceived, and then stores that information along with any visual memory of the object. Thus, if you are shown a map of the United States turned on its side (as illustrated in Chapter 6), it is extremely difficult to recognize; this is because the map is ordinarily perceived by the orientation of unusual shapes such as Florida and California which are no longer immediately recognizable and because the basic outline of the country was originally learned with the characteristic shapes of Canada and the Gulf Coast as the top and bottom, and the California Baja and Maine/Florida coast as the left and right sides. The same principle of perception goes for photographs of even the most familiar faces which cannot be recognized upside down because we are so used to information coming from the top of the image as being hair, not chin.

So basic is this perceptual organization that it is assumed to correspond to the nature of reality itself. In a fascinating experiment, however, subjects were given goggles which distorted perception in various ways—turned things upside down, for example, or curved everything severely to the left or right. For the first two weeks of the experiment, the subjects of course had extreme difficulty in recognizing features of the environment and in maneuvering around them. After this, however, they achieved a new sense of reality in which what had been upside down now became right side up. The brain had relearned top and bottom, left and right sides for objects which could then be perceived perfectly normally.

Even more intriguing, however, is what happened when, after becoming accustomed to the distorting goggles, the subjects were allowed to see "normally" again. Their response without the goggles was precisely the same as when the goggles were first put on—that the world was upside down, bent to the left, and so on. Again it took two weeks for the brain to adapt.

In addition to the organizing process that learns top and bottom and right and left sides of a form, there is one that "fills in" the missing elements of a shape that is perceived to be "incomplete" based on what the brain's model says it ought to be. If you are shown a circle with a piece blocked out (see Chapter 6), you almost automatically complete the circle in your brain—to the point where you may not even recognize that the process has taken place.

Still another set of "rules" helps distinguish objects from their backgrounds, so that the lines representing a cube, for example, are perceived as not only being joined together into a single object but are also separate from and move independently of the background. This kind of perceptual organization is so strong that it is virtually impossible, even when one concentrates on the task, to compress foreground and background together so they can be seen on a single plane.

Many of these perceptual patterns are the "rules" of Gestalt psychology which were explored to some extent in the discussion of the development of sensory systems (Chapter 4) and will be looked at again in Chapter 8. The important consideration here is that any visual signal intended by the sender to convey a message with color or form is bound to be affected by how it is perceived by the receiver's sensory system.

This issue is fundamental in communications since the message intended by the sender may not be what is perceived by the receiver. For though the physiological process of vision and the basic models of perceptual organization work unconsciously and are independent of intent, conscious choice must also play a major role in how things are perceived. This consciousness was a major component of the teachings of Don Juan, the Yaqui medicine man of Carlos Castaneda's books, who could apparently control very accurately not only what he wanted others to see (and not see) of himself but also how he saw others. But to a lesser extent, this kind of control is exercised continuously in daily life.

Very, very few signals and messages, it turns out, rely on inherent perceptual processes rather than those which are culturally learned (and can therefore be unlearned just as easily as goggle-distorted vision becomes the new norm). The color red is *not* an inherent, universal symbol for "stop" any more than body tattooing is an inherently attractive practice. Indeed, why should the language of sensory communication be any more universal than words themselves?

One of the clearest examples are the "colors" white and black. In the West, based on cultural history dating back beyond individual memory, they have always stood for good and evil—the color made up of all the other colors versus the total absence of color, purity and heaven versus damnation and the blackness of hell, and so forth. It always comes as a surprise to those in the West, therefore, to learn that this symbolism is anything but universal. Black is certainly not an evil color to the black-skinned peoples of the world. The ancient Egyptians saw black—the color of the fertile mud of the Nile, the source of life—as a "positive" color.

Equally interesting are the responses of Oriental societies to black and white. Contrary to Western practices, Japanese funerary garments are made of white cloth and Japanese coffins are draped in white. This ties in with observations about Japanese children made by Faye Goldberg of the University of Chicago. While children brought up in Western cultures associate "good objects" with the color white, and assume that the "good" objects will always be found in a white box, Japanese children are different. Although they agree with Western children as to which objects are "good" and which "bad," they make no assumption that the good objects will always be found in white boxes.

These differences are not just true for black and white. In Buddhist religion, yellow is the color of death. And red, the color which we so automatically assume is a universal sign for "stop, danger" has virtually as many meanings around the world as there are cultures. Even in the West, red hasn't always meant danger; the Alchemists cherished the rosy cross as if it were white.

Is there something about the color blue that makes it inherently special or sacred, just as there appears to be something special about the number seven? At first glance it would appear so. Americans prefer blue over every other color, according to Philip Knowles of Western Washington University, along with choosing the number seven over every other number. But in a crosscultural test conducted by Peter Schickinger of the Albert-Ludwigs University in Freiburg, West Germany, in which fourteen colors are presented and experimental subjects asked to rate them according to excitement, value, and power, Spaniards found white to be the most pleasing color of the fourteen.

As for inherent emotional properties of colors—the reason American interior designers turn to blues and greens as "soothing"— Germans find clearer, lighter colors stimulating while Spaniards find them calming, and Germans find dark blue calming although Spaniards do not. In another study, done by Leo Darakis of the University of Paris, in which the galvanic skin response was used to measure excitement, French college students found purple to be the most arousing of the six colors they were presented with; green, violet, and yellow seemed to diminish arousal.

Not only does color preference shift as easily as languages and geographical boundaries, but it appears to change even throughout the life of an individual. Among third grade American children, yellow, orange, green, and blue are considered "happy colors" while red, brown, and black are "sad." By the time Americans reach college age, however, the emotional connotation of blue has changed from happy to sad. Among Czech youth, according to

Czech researcher Maria Busniakova, there also appears to be a shift in preferred color saturation, with younger people preferring bright, highly-saturated colors while university students prefer more pastel-like shades.

Even the classic notion that some colors such as red appear to "advance" and are "hot" while others such as blue appear to "recede" and are "cool" is not proving out in the light of new color research. The operative factor in advancing and receding appears to be the contrast between the colors and their backgrounds rather than the colors themselves, according to Mario Farne and Francesco Campione of the University of Bologna, Italy; colors offering the most contrast appear to "stand out" (advance) more than colors that blend better with the background.

In this context, it is interesting to note the major importance of color in the way things taste. A little tasteless, odorless green food coloring added to oatmeal makes it virtually unpalatable to most. Red coloring, on the other hand, seems far more acceptable and is a major component of the food industry's attempt to make foods look more appetizing. Soy bean paste, variously colored reddish or whitish, can be made to strongly suggest beef or chicken to vegetarians although it, itself, has almost no taste.

Thus, conscious choices about color and form obviously comprise a major part of communication. And yet, despite all our suggestions that most of this nonverbal communication is a learned, cultural phenomenon, there is, indeed, a kind of communication that takes place between individuals which *is* based on innate, instinctual, universal meanings. This is the language of the unconscious signal in which neither the sender nor the receiver is aware that communication is happening.

In cultures that maintain eye contact during conversations, a massive amount of signaling is taking place just in the actions of the face (eyes, nose, mouth) alone. This begins in early childhood when the communication between parent and child is based on the pitch of the voice and the expression of the eyes and mouth. The non-verbal communication becomes so complex, in fact, that some have suggested that a child develops spoken language to avoid the frustration of not being able to share this complex communication with others who don't understand the infant's facial expressions the way the mother does.

In later life, the adult face is just as expressive, although more accessible forms of communication make it easy to ignore. Part of the face's ability to signal emotions has to do with its asymmetry and the fact that the left and right halves are seldom saying the same thing. This is confirmed by taking a photograph of a face (see Figure F in Chapter 6), splitting it in half, and then using a photographic process to create two new photographs made up of two left halves and two right halves. Almost invariably, people will say that the image composed of the two right-sided halves looks more like the whole face than the left-halves composite. The right side is, in a sense, the more "public" side.

But while the right side is busy conveying the emotions that are more conscious and that we want others to see, the left side is working on far more personal thoughts—the true emotions that are being felt. Using the same procedure with the split faces, subjects in an experiment by Harold Sackeim, Reuben Gur, and Marcel Saucy at the University of Pennsylvania felt that the left-sided composites expressed emotions far more intensely for most of the emotions that the face is capable of expressing. And all this is apparently reversed in left-handed people, who tend to use the right side of the face for expressing most emotions.

Part of this is purely physiological: one side of the face is often smaller than the other, and therefore seems to express more intense emotions because the emotions are more "concentrated" on that side. Another difference in left-right face size is that the muscles controlling facial movements differ from one side of the face to the other, as do the fatty deposits that form the facial contours and even the bundles of nerves which carry information that makes the muscles react.

But more than simply reflecting physical differences, the two sides of the face may represent a division as fundamental as the structure of the brain itself. For despite the high school biology notion that the body is bilaterally symmetrical, the brain certainly isn't. The left half of the brain (which controls the right side of the body and also the muscles in the right side of the face) has far more area devoted to analytical activities—speech, logic, and so forth; the right hemisphere (controlling the left side of the body and face) has more area devoted to non-analytical activities such as emotions, pattern perception, "feelings." (This is why left-handed people, in whom the right hemisphere is presumably more dominant, are sometimes thought to be "special" or "gifted" in artistic endeavors, while "righties" are thought to make the best mathematicians.)

These differences are obviously manifested in the way the two sides of the face express emotion. The more outward, public feelings, representing what we *want* others to see, are expressed on the right side of the face (controlled by the left hemisphere). The more inward, emotional feelings, those which we might not want to show to others, are expressed on the left side of the face (controlled by the brain's right hemisphere).

These differences also have an effect on the person viewing our face. Emotions which are expressed on the right, public side are in the perceiver's left visual field in a face-to-face encounter. And the left visual field is interpreted by the brain's right hemisphere—the area reserved for pattern recognition and essentially nonverbal activities. The less-public left side of the speaker's face, on the other hand, is perceived by the viewer's left hemisphere, the inferior of the two halves when it comes to pattern recognition.

As an experiment, try sometime to consciously pay attention to the left side of a person's face as he or she speaks. This will involve, of course, breaking the normal viewing habit and looking "across" the speaker's face, and the speaker may find your gaze disconcerting. But you will probably be able to notice that the nonpublic left side is the side conveying what the speaker is really thinking about.

Another difference in the two brain hemispheres—that the left is perhaps better at receiving positive and the right at receiving negative emotional signals—may account for yet another difference between left- and right-sided facial expressions. A study by Patricia Reuter-Lorenz and Richard Davidson of the University of Toronto showed that happiness is apparently registered more quickly when appearing in the right visual field (perceived by the left hemisphere) of the listener. Sadness is the exact opposite process.

Besides these differences in muscular activity, another unconscious signaling system of the face is pupil size, a completely involuntary measure of our apparent interest or disinterest in, pleasure in or dislike of, what we hear and see. Pupil size, of course, is controlled by a completely separate part of the brain than the visual cortex, so that even if brain damage has caused the inability to "see" anything, pupils will still react when a light is shone on them. But somehow a link is made between the two brain centers so that looking at a pleasurable object—a picture of food, for instance—causes the pupils to dilate within seconds. The face is therefore an open book of true emotional response.

Others' reading of the signals, too, happens unconsciously. For we react strongly to another's pupil size even though we are completely unaware of it. In one experiment, performed by Eckhard Hess of the University of Chicago, two groups of men were shown identical photographs of a female model except that one photograph was retouched to make the pupils appear smaller and one to make them appear larger (illustrated in Figure B in Chapter 6). Unaware of the retouching, the group that saw the photograph with the larger pupils felt the woman was somehow warmer, friendlier, more receptive, while the other group found the same woman with smaller pupils to be unfriendly and cold. But the experimental subjects weren't even aware of the difference between the two photographs.

Given a choice between four photographs—a man with wide or narrow pupils and a woman with wide or narrow pupils—both men and women will almost invariably choose as the most friendly the photo of the member of the opposite sex with large pupils. But although men showed almost no preference between either wide- or narrow-pupiled males, women responded unfavorably to the photo of another woman with wide pupils. In interacting with actual females whose pupils had been dilated or constricted with drops, however, women subjects described the former as "open" and "soft" and complained that the latter were "cold" and "hard."

Interest or disinterest, of course, is measured by whether the viewer himself or herself shows any increase in pupil size when viewing another face. And this interplay—registering that the other person has wide pupils, unconsciously interpreting this as a sign of interest in you, unconsciously increasing the diameter of your own pupils in response, and signaling this back to the other person whose pupils become even wider—may be part of the biological explanation that accounts for that magical moment when we meet someone who "really turns us on." In this light, one must question whether the Moslem custom of covering a woman's face except for her eyes is as effective a deterrent of sexuality as is supposed.

As might be predicted, male homosexuals have an opposite response to the pictures of women with wide and narrow pupils, showing a preference for women with narrower pupils (presumably less sexually threatening), according to Thomas Simms of the University of Toronto. Even more interesting, however, is that heterosexual males who consider themselves more interested in sexual encounters than in lasting relationships (a Don-Juan-like attitude), also show the same response and favor the woman with narrower pupils (again perhaps rejecting the sexual threat of the interested woman).

Facial expressions and pupil size are not the only forms of nonverbal, unconscious communication, of course. Lately there have been new studies suggesting that, despite the supposedly arbitrary nature of the relationship between color and emotions, color itself has a physiological effect on the body. One of the more startling revelations in this area is that bubble-gum pink, according to observations made by Paul Boccumini of the San Bernardino County Probation Department, apparently has an almost instantaneous calming influence on children and adolescents—to the point where it is being used instead of restraining jackets in mental hospitals and correctional facilities. Violent children placed in pink rooms often fall asleep within minutes. Another study, done at the University of Northern Colorado, shows that men placed in a red room have more strength in their arm muscles than those placed in blue or pink rooms—perhaps because the color red brings out irritation and aggressive tendencies. Another explanation for these phenomena, however, is that the color actually affects the body in the same way as heat and cold—a hypothesis we will explore in Chapter 9.

With all these recent discoveries about communication and the visual process at hand, it is tempting to think that we finally have an answer to some of mankind's oldest questions, both psychological and physiological. Science may, indeed, be close. But even with all the research and the knowledge, there is still a fundamental piece of the puzzle that is missing. If one imagined a picture of what scientists suggest is the actual image perceived by the brain based on the rod cells of the retina, added color information from the cones, factored in the associative memories which the object conjures up, defined it with the shapes of Gestalt psychology, and integrated it with what is known of consciousness itself, the image would still look nothing like what we experience in real-life vision. The link between "I see" (visually) and "I see" (conceptually) still remains a profoundly unsolvable mystery.

Chapter Six
A Guide to Visual Perception

As explained in previous chapters and later in Chapter 8, the visual sense is a highly complex combination of neural receptors, increasingly complex brain processing, conscious decisions, unconscious patterning, attentiveness, and so forth. The final explanation of how, exactly, the brain organizes visual data into a form that corresponds with the reality outside the body is still somewhat of a mystery, although the processes are beginning to be understood.

In the following pages we present some of the most revealing images scientists now use to demonstrate what is known about visual perception. Some are familiar—optical illusions, for example, which show the ambiguity of perception that occurs when one perceptual pattern conflicts with another or when foreground and background cannot be easily distinguished. Disoriented figures illustrate how the brain works to assign top and bottom, left and right values to an image no matter what the position of the head. Retouched photographs clearly show the importance of facial expressions in communications. And other images reveal clues about how various visual signals interact within the nervous system.

In most cases, the images themselves are quite simple. But the processes they reveal are those at the core of the modern understanding of vision.

FIGURE A: FACE/VASE

Distinguishing foreground from background is a major component of perception. Normal cues include the relative sizes of the foreground and background. Color helps, too. In this figure, however, normal cues are distorted. Presented with two equally valid explanations of the contours, the brain shifts back and forth between seeing the white areas as a foreground vase and seeing the black areas as foreground faces.

FIGURE B: PUPIL SIZE

What are your reactions to this person? Shown the upper photograph, most men thought the woman was friendly, warm, open,
receptive. Shown the bottom photograph, men said the woman was
cold, hard, unfriendly. The photographs are identical except that
the top one was retouched so the pupils appear wider, indicating
the importance of this unconscious, nonverbal cue in communications.

FIGURE C: SQUARE AND DIAMOND

These two figures are identical except that one is rotated 90 degrees relative to the other. Psychologically, however, they are completely different. One is perceived as a square, the other as a diamond. Tilting the head does not make the diamond turn into a square or the square into a diamond. At the same time that information is being processed about a figure's lines and contours, they are assigned values such as "top," "bottom," and "sides" which remain as part of the brain's object description.

FIGURE D: TRIANGULAR ILLUSION

This optical illusion relies on the brain's desire to make individual parts of an object make sense even though the total object is completely fictitious. Thus, the relationship of each corner of the triangle "works" according to the perceptual rules of Gestalt psychology, whereas the illusion of dimensionality which the individual corners should create cannot take place.

FIGURE E: MACH BANDS

After staring at the circle for a few seconds, you should see two
rings—a more intense band of black just inside the circle and a
more intense band of white just outside it. The rest of the black and
white areas appear duller because lateral inhibition of the nerves
reduces neural impulses except at the boundaries of a form where
the full nerve impulse is allowed to get through. Presumably this
phenomenon helps in distinguishing contours of objects from the
background.

FIGURE F: SPLIT FACE

Both the top and bottom images on page 126 were made from the original photograph shown above, except that the top one is composed of two right halves of the face while the one at the bottom is composed of two left halves.

In face-to-face encounters, the right side of a person's face is perceived by the right hemisphere of the viewer's brain, the part most adept at facial recognition. Thus, it is not surprising that the top image, made up of the right halves, looks "more like the person" than the face made up of the left halves.

Even though the right side of the face is the more "public" side, emotions are expressed more intently on the left, or "private" side.

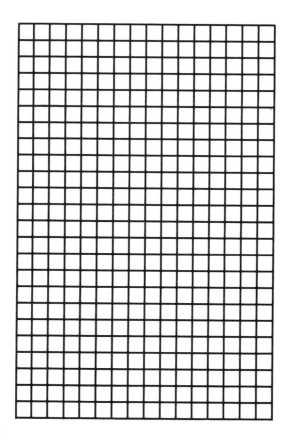

FIGURE G: BATHROOM TILES

One of the properties of perception is that it insists on creating "meaningful" patterns in a figure like this—reminiscent of the tiles on a bathroom floor. Besides pinpointing possible retinal damage (if some areas appear darker than others, if blank spots appear, etc.) the figure will begin transforming itself into regular patterns when stared at for a few moments. All the lines are, of course, of equal thickness and there is nothing in the drawing other than a perfectly regular grid.

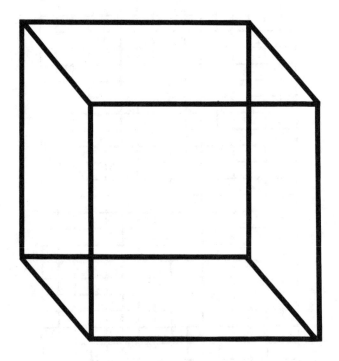

FIGURE H: REVERSING CUBE

This cube offers a clear example of the optical illusion known as reversible (or ambiguous) figures. Because the cube can be seen in two different ways and because there are no cues that tell the brain which is more "correct," we see both. The two interpretations are never seen simultaneously, and the brain seems to switch back and forth between the two apparently randomly. The change can be consciously brought about, however, if one picks a corner with recognizable features that will suddenly bring the shape into focus.

FIGURE I: YOUNG WOMAN/OLD WOMAN

This reversible figure is especially interesting because people usually see one face quite distinctly at first, but have trouble recognizing the other until it is pointed out. Once both have been seen, however, the brain can be directed to look at either by recognizing a particular point in the illustration that is somehow pivotal. For the authors, this point is the young woman's chin, which becomes the old woman's nose.

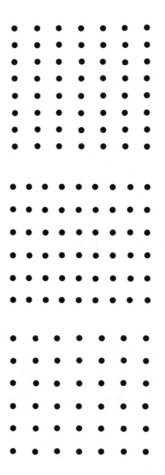

FIGURE J: DOT PATTERNS

This is an example of the perceptual patterning that organizes regularly spaced elements into regular patterns. Depending on how they are spaced, the dots are arranged in either vertical or horizontal patterns in the top two examples. In the bottom example, however, where the spacing is perfectly equal, the dots are seen as either horizontal or vertical, and alternate between the two. But horizontal and vertical are never seen at the same time.

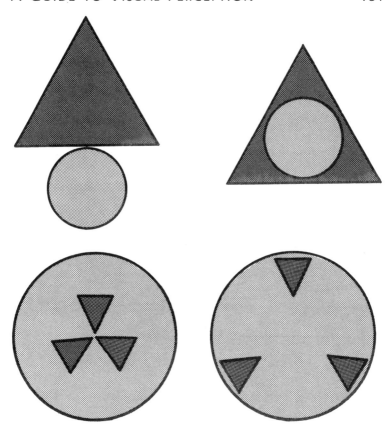

FIGURE K: BEHAVIOR TEST

These two sets of figures are similar to those used to self test such behavioral traits as sexual preferences. The idea is to pick which of the top two and bottom two figures you prefer. Then you evaluate the results—inward, introverted behavior versus extroverted behavior, a preference for romantic partnerships rather than group activities, and so on. However, test designers often overlook the role that left and right positioning may have. Is it possible many people will choose the patterns on the left simply because that is the side most connected with the right hemisphere and the brain's pattern processing center, not because they actually prefer them?

FIGURE L: RABBIT/DUCK

Another well-known reversible figure. The rabbit's head and the duck's head are quite clearly seen, although because the viewer's eyes must shift their center of attention from the right to the left sides of the image the two heads cannot be seen at once.

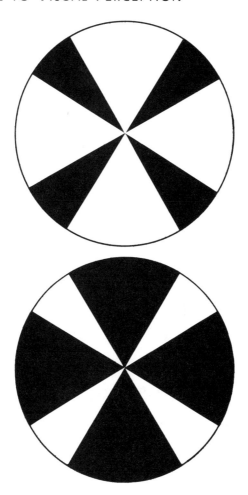

FIGURE M: MALTESE CROSS

Part of the ability to distinguish foreground from background is that in a figure such as this the larger areas are more likely to be perceived as the background while the smaller areas are more likely to be seen as foreground objects. Sometimes the eye will pick the larger area to be seen as the Maltese cross, but more often it is the small segments that make up the cross shape.

FIGURE N: DIVIDED CIRCLE

This instantly created reversible figure is simply an arbitrary line drawn through a circle. It is seen either as a wavelike shape coming from the left and covering the circle, or coming from the right and covering the other half—but not both at the same time. The two contours are so radically different that it is hard to imagine that the "in" and "out" pieces are actually created by the same line.

FIGURE O: MISSING PIECES

The brain's pattern-recognition models function even without specific visual information. In the figure on the upper left, for example, the eye creates a white triangular form that intersects with the lines to create a "Star of David." In the upper drawing on the right, the same imaginary triangle is formed, only this time black because of the background. In the two drawings on the bottom, the imaginary lines of the triangle are curved, with the pattern controlled by the shapes of the cut-out circles.

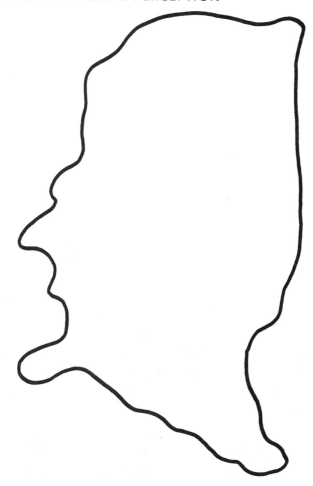

FIGURE P: MAP

This disoriented figure is simply a map of the United States turned 89 degrees on its side. But the image is so unrecognizable that it is seen as a stylized face of a man with a beard—perhaps the original reason for the emergence of the "Uncle Sam" figure. Older maps that show north as pointing to the side are often completely unrecognizable to the modern user for whom "north," "up," and "top" are virtually synonymous.

FIGURE Q: ANGELS AND DEVILS

This drawing by the artist M. C. Escher is a classic example of foreground/background reversal. By concentrating on either the white areas or the black areas, completely different patterns can be seen within the circle. Escher was also a master with other optical illusions such as "impossible figures."

Chapter Seven
Making Scents

If we were to end Chapter 5's description of how the senses signal and receive signals in human communications without further discussion, it would appear that the blind are all but insensitive to most of the nonverbal communications that go on between people, and that those who are deaf and blind lose whatever small amount of information is left. On the contrary, however, those blind and deaf from birth can clearly distinguish one person from another as they approach. Without vision or hearing, in fact, we would all still probably be acutely sensitive to others of the species. The mechanism by which this is done is the nose, and the sense of smell.

As is true for the other senses, there is a certain component to smelling that can be very consciously manipulated. This is the part that has spawned an industry in toiletries which spends over a billion dollars a year in advertising alone—directed toward an American public that seems to have an insatiable appetite for items that will either prevent body odors from developing (underarm deodorants, foot odor powders, vaginal douches, etc.) or mask them when they do (perfumes, aftershave lotions, etc.). A whole separate group of products keep the mouth and breath smelling fresh. And personal care products are separate again from the enormous variety of detergents and deodorizers to clean, sanitize, and make fresh-smelling everything from cat boxes to laundry to carpets.

In the case of the perfume industry, at least, this commerce in scents caters to a seemingly timeless desire to anoint the body with unguents and oils either to attract members of the opposite sex or to make oneself more presentable in public (the latter practice clearly originated in days when the luxury of daily bathing with indoor plumbing was less available).

Like the other senses, part of the sense of smell is conscious, and it can be trained to be more discriminating. Industry professionals can indeed train their noses to remember certain fragrances so they can be recreated in a perfume laboratory. Given a certain amount of practice, in fact, virtually anyone can become more sensitive to perfumes and odors, and can be trained to pick out the components of more complex aromas—the vanilla, musk, cinnamon, rose, carnation, and other compounds commonly used in commercial perfumes, for instance.

Smell also shares a common feature with the other senses in being somewhat influenced by the prevailing culture. Just as most Americans don't recognize the attractiveness of stretched lips and necks, so we don't appreciate the odor of rancid fat which some cultures use as an attractant and to smooth down their hair.

Americans and Europeans, of course, have perfume preferences of their own. And, like the color preferences described earlier, scent preference is linked with age. Teenage boys, for instance, seem to prefer somewhat recognizable fragrances such as vanilla- and lavender-based scents. Teenage girls, their sense of smell apparently heightened at puberty, also go in for the recognizable fragrances, often sweet smells such as strawberry. After adolescence, tastes change toward the more sophisticated fragrances and away from the sweet and recognizable. Musk, a substance secreted by some animals to attract members of the opposite sex and also apparently a human sexual attractant, becomes an important ingredient. Later in life, as the sex drive diminishes, the ability to smell becomes less and less important and the number of smell-sensing cells decreases (dropping off even more sharply at menopause); preference again turns back toward the flowery and the sweet. The diminished ability to smell may also account for the fact that older people sometimes overdo perfume application.

But there is more to smell than this conscious control, something even more powerful as a communications vehicle. For actually the sense of smell is not very conscious at all.

Vision, as we mentioned earlier, can create in fine detail a whole scene out of a completely imaginary description. But try to *imagine* the smell of hot apple pie. Not the taste, not the way it looks, but the smell. Try to add the scents of the wildflowers to the scene in the sunlit field described earlier. Try to reconstruct the smell of a favorite perfume. Or the odor of a skunk. It's a property of the sense of smell itself that although it allows us to remember *that* something was smelled, we cannot summon up into conscious memory *how* it smelled.

Nor, unlike the well-developed vocabulary for describing what is seen, is there a way of talking about what is smelled. One quantifies odors by saying they are "strong" or "weak." One evaluates them as smelling "good" or "bad." One compares them to well-recognized scents in the natural world such as "lemony" or "piney." And one resorts to describing the associations which the scents evoke, such as "manly," "feminine," or "wild."

But what does pine really smell like? There are no words in the vocabulary of any human language that can communicate the sensation to another who has not experienced it directly. And there is no way of consciously stimulating the memory of smell in the same way that can be done with visual or auditory information.

In short, the abstractions of language and thought and cognition that make conscious communication possible about the other senses apparently don't apply to the world of smells. The chemical sense of smell and the ability to describe what it perceives seem less developed, almost primitive.

On the other hand, the sensation of smell provides signals between members of the species that may be at least as important as, if not more than, visual and auditory data. When meeting someone who strongly attracts us sexually, we say "It's chemical." In the purest sense of the word, it may be exactly that—the receipt, through the nose, of powerful sexual signals released by a potential partner who is ready, willing, and able, signals which the transmitter might even find embarrassing if they were ever made conscious.

Similarly, one talks about being able to "smell fear" and having a "nose for danger." Is this the vestige of a signaling mechanism left over from a more primitive stage of life when threatened individuals released scents that may have alerted others that danger was nearby? Or possibly been used to scare off attackers? Is this what we know today as "nervous perspiration"—the unpleasant odor that affects some people during crisis situations and is somehow different from ordinary sweat?

It has even been suggested by some, as mentioned in Chapter 4, that the sense of smell may be associated with the experience of déjà vu, the feeling that we've been there before or experienced the event before or have seen the place before, but can't remember where or how. Could this experience be brought about because a scent we unconsciously pick up in the present activates a deeply buried, unconscious memory we have of the same scent experienced in the past? In other words, we may actually have a memory for scents after all, but one that is not stored in the same way that more conscious memories are filed.

In fact, the human sense of smell is not only concerned with these rather basic, gut-level emotions, it *is* an altogether primitive sense, probably the single most powerful link still binding our species to the unconscious, primitive, animal-like existence left behind when language, reason, and consciousness were developed. Early evolutionary life forms such as reptiles, for example, had a special set of nerve endings in the brain reserved for olfaction, which made contact with the nerves governing the most instinctual types of behavior. As evolution progressed, the "reptilian" brain, together with the olfactory sense and its nervous system connections, was incorporated into the brain structure of emerging life forms such as birds and mammals. And the selfsame reptilian brain with its olfactory sense and central nervous system pathways, now deeply buried within the increasing amount of brain area devoted to thinking activity, was passed along first to primitive mammals and then, via primates, to man. The human brain of today still carries within it a multimillion-year-old evolutionary legacy of the reptilian brain and its olfactory bulb where nerve endings from the nose terminate.

What's more, the connection between the sense of smell and visceral, unconscious reactions has also followed the same evolutionary course. The identical "reptilian" part of the brain that incorporates olfaction also contains the nerve center that controls involuntary, nonconscious muscular activity such as breathing, heartbeat, pupil size, and genital erections; the neurophysiological association between sex and the sense of smell is apparently one that goes back all the way to the beginning of human evolution itself.

There is also a psychological corollary to all this. As Sigmund Freud and Carl Jung observed, as human civilization has progressed from primitive life in the cave to modern life as we know it, more and more of our primitive, instinctual nature has had to be left behind in favor of the higher goals of intellect, culture, and society. Freud and Jung noted that this process of "leaving something behind" has meant a rejection of the unconscious mind and all the fantasy and dreamlike qualities that it represents.

It is not at all surprising, therefore, to find not only that smells are not part of consciousness, but that they are often loudly rejected as a possible source of information and communication—totally unlike the utter trust placed on visual cues. The smells of sweat and urine and feces and sexual secretions, so important in the world of animals, so vital for mating and food gathering and parental care and warning others, are almost deliberately set aside in the effort to be "civilized." And though musk and civet and ambergris—all derived from the scent glands of other animals—are used to attract members of our species, our own body odors are covered up with a fierce intensity.

It is also not surprising to find that despite the importance smell has in human communications, it has not been the subject of extensive scientific inquiry. Science, as we have noted, tends to reflect the mores of the time, and olfaction and smells were simply not discussed in polite circles. Consequently, until very recently, there has been almost no investigation of the human ability to detect odors.

Much of what we do know about olfaction comes from observation of the behavior of other species, in which detection of smells can often be as important to survival as sights and sounds are to humans. This is obviously true when it comes to detecting possible food sources. But it is equally the case for detecting pheromones—chemical signals used for intraspecies communication. Mating, defense, warning, identification, and parent/child bonding are just the top of a long list of essential activities either controlled by or influenced by pheromonal signaling in many animal species.

In fish, for example, this kind of signaling serves as a warning. When a predator bites into a minnow, the minnow's skin releases chemicals into the water that frighten away other minnows, preventing them from succumbing to the same fate. The mechanism may also help curtail cannibalism, preventing the mother from digesting more of her babies after she has injured the first.

Many species obviously use the scent of food as an important way to locate it, and birds such as the albatross, which use the smell of fish oils floating on the water's surface as a guide, have much better-developed olfactory organs than do other birds that tend to rely on sight. But some species, such as ants, also create their own chemical signals to tell other ants where the food is located. Worker ants lay down a scent trail wherever they go, exciting other ants to follow them to the source of food, and as more and more ants join the trail, the signal becomes stronger and stronger, attracting more and more ants. Once the food supply is gone, however, the ants begin looking in another direction and the scent trail evaporates within a minute or two so more ants are not attracted.

Self-defense is another important area in which odors play a major role, enabling animals to detect the presence of predators before it is too late. Probably the most interesting example occurs in rattlesnakes, which assume the classic coiled posture when threatened, then lash out with venomous fangs. One of the rattler's enemies, however, is the king snake, which is immune to rattlesnake venom. When it is confronted by a king snake, therefore, the rattler takes a different course of action; it lays its head flat to the ground and attempts to back away. Even if the king snake follows, the rattler will not try to use its venom, but will arch its body into a loop and attempt to club the king snake to death. The rattler's identification of the kingsnake by its chemical odor alone can be enough to trigger this behavior. If placed in a cage that has recently housed a king snake, the rattler will become visibly distressed and assume the exact same defensive postures it would if a king snake were really present.

The most intriguing examples of odor perception, however, are those relating to various aspects of sexuality—counterparts of the human "It's chemical" response. The onset of puberty in a female mouse, for example, can be brought on by her sensing pheromones in the urine of male mice, while it can be retarded by a different set of pheromones present in the urine of other adult female mice. The obvious effect is to make a female mouse more able to breed when male mice are present.

In rats, experiments have been performed in which the olfactory bulbs (both main and accessory) are removed in six-day-old females. In almost every case, the vagina failed to open for at least ten days longer than in normal rats. Growth of the uterus and ovaries in these rats also lagged behind that of control rats. The fluctuations in lutenizing hormone, normally present in the pituitary gland before vaginal opening, were absent. And ovarian corpora lutea, the cells that develop into eggs, were also almost always absent. All these phenomena occurred simply because of the removal of the olfactory bulbs, with their obviously powerful influence on the sex organs.

Development of the sex organs is not the only connection between sex and smell, however. Sex plays a vital role for some species in mate selection. In rhinoceroses, for example, which are notoriously short-sighted and cannot always tell the difference between an automobile and an eligible mate by sight alone, the male rhino uses the pheromones present in the urine and dung of a fertile female to lead him to her. Rhinos also rely on pheromones to mark trails and the boundaries of their territories.

Even among species as "advanced" in evolution as monkeys, researchers can point to powerful response mechanisms based on smell. In one test, female rhesus monkeys were treated with estrogen, the female hormone, in differing amounts. Male monkeys could tell by smell which female had received the greatest amount of the hormone, and always chose her to copulate with. (Estrogen is released in most mammals as the female comes into heat and becomes most fertile.) The corollary is also true: a male monkey deprived of its olfactory abilities through surgical removal has an extremely difficult time mating at all.

Experiments with squirrel monkeys yield much the same results. Normally these animals display an erect phallus as a form of greeting, courtship, aggression, and other forms of social interaction. When, in experiments, the nerve pathways from the two outer, "thinking" portions of the brain are interrupted, the monkeys will still have erections. On the other hand, when impulses from the interior, "reptilian" part of the brain where the olfactory sense is located are experimentally interrupted, the monkeys no longer display erections.

What all these experiments demonstrate is that, in virtually every species from the most primitive reptile to the most advanced primate, the reptilian part of the brain, the part responsible for the olfactory sense, is involved with the most essential aspects of social interaction, including sexuality. But what of humans? Do our "deeply buried" and "deeply rooted" instincts actually reside in an inner part of our brains, connected there with the perception of odors and pheromones?

In humans, smell obviously plays a major role in such basics as eating, warning of danger, simple social interactions, and so forth. As Robert Henkin at the Georgetown Taste and Smell Clinic has shown so vividly, those who cannot smell have a difficult time with many of life's everyday activities. Nineteen percent of his patients had been involved in a major fire but were unaware of the smoke; 16 percent had been exposed to lethal amounts of natural gas without knowing it; 25 percent had had food burn on the stove and had only realized it by visual clues or being told about it; and almost a third had had the unfortunate experience of eating spoiled food or drink without the usual bad smell and taste warning. "Smell blind" people worry constantly about body odors, about serving bad food to others, about many things which most others take for granted.

Perhaps more important, those who experience a loss of smell as a result of blows to the head, severe colds, allergies, and the like, also often develop an associated loss of interest in sex. As the sense of smell returns to normal, so does their sexuality.

Even those with normal olfaction think that smell is very important to sex, however. On a scale of 1 to 10, smell is ranked amazingly high as a source of sexual stimulation—as high as 9.9 to those living on the East Coast of the United States (although Californians rate it considerably lower, just over a 7 on the average). To support these observations, breakthrough research is beginning to discover that the sense of smell does indeed play a significant role in human interaction and human sexuality. But the key to understanding how smells function may involve far more than the olfactory sense. Researchers have discovered the existence of a separate sensory system in many species which is thought to be especially sensitive to pheromones. In these animals, a small mushroom-shaped body can be found lodged within the nose near the roof of the mouth, buried within the cartilage that separates the two nostrils. Called the vomeronasal organ (from vomer, the name of the small bone that forms the lower part of the nasal septum), this sensory organ makes neural connections to the accessory olfactory bulb (which is distinguishable from the main olfactory bulb which handles smells) and from there to areas of the brain which are also separate from those to which the olfactory nerves project.

The existence of the vomeronasal system has been particularly well documented in lizards and other reptiles. While many reptiles use this sensory system for foodgathering and other purposes, its function in mating is clearly revealed in experiments with a species of iguanid lizards native to the Arizona canyons. As has been known for some time, the tongue flicking behavior of snakes and lizards is a prime method by which reptiles receive information about the world around them, for it is one of the animal's ways of sensing chemical substances that are left by other reptiles and by virtually every other living thing. Molecules, including those comprising pheromones, are literally scooped up by the lizard's tongue, then carried into the mouth and deposited in ducts leading to the vomeronasal organ. Smells, on the other hand, enter through the reptile's nostrils and are directed to the main olfactory bulb. Thus the difference between detecting pheromones and other chemicals through the vomeronasal system and detecting odors is as pronounced as the difference between detecting odors and detecting tastes. Different sensory systems are involved. In the natural environment, lizards are continually probing the air for signals, making more tongue extrusions when the environment is unfamiliar, presumably so they can learn more about it, including whether others of the species are nearby.

The experiments done in Arizona also specifically demonstrated the role of the vomeronasal system in the lizard's sexual behavior. A quadrant of four "pens" was set up on the canyon floor, approximating the natural environment for the lizards. Leaving one of the pens vacant, an adult male lizard, an adult female lizard, and juvenile females which had not yet reached maturity were placed into the other three pens respectively and allowed to live there for several days—long enough for them to leave behind whatever pheromones they would normally secrete. These lizards were then removed.

The significant part of the experiment began when another group of lizards was introduced to the enclosure one at a time and allowed to choose which pen they would enter. In dramatically increased numbers, the adult male lizards chose the pen in which the adult female lizard had been allowed to live. Not only were they attracted to this area, but the number of tongue extrusions increased there, too, indicating that there was something worth exploring in the environment—a nearby female.

Further, the male lizards, provoked only by the presence of female lizard pheromones, began immediately to exhibit sexual behavior, including the characteristic rubbing of the hind quarters on the ground, presumably releasing male pheromones of their own which might stimulate females and make them more receptive.

In another experiment, a researcher severed either the olfactory nerve or the vomeronasal nerve in two groups of male snakes which had previously been sexually active. In the group in which the olfactory nerve was cut, all the snakes courted normally and three of ten copulated. In the group of ten whose vomeronasal nerves were cut, however, none mated and only one courted (it was subsequently discovered that the experimental surgery had left some of its vomeronasal nerves intact). So, in reptiles at least, the vomeronasal system and sexuality are definitely connected while olfaction and sexuality are connected to a much lesser degree.

Many species of mammals, too, have well-developed vomeronasal systems. Common house cats as well as deer, horses, and many other species exhibit what is called the Flehmen response—a characteristic curling of the upper lip, wrinkling of the nose, and throwing back of the head—the purpose of which is to direct a stream of air up against the nerve receptors for the vomeronasal system. The vomeronasal system plays the same role for these animals as it does in reptiles, acting as a prime stimulant for sexual responses and other forms of interaction. What is proving to be the case is that it is not the sense of smell as much as it is the vomeronasal response to pheromones that brings about these activities.

The experiment described above in which snakes' olfactory and vomeronasal nerves were cut, can, for example, be duplicated on hamsters. When male hamsters' olfactory and vomeronasal nerves are experimentally cut, mating behavior and copulation are eliminated in every single experimental animal. Destroying the olfactory tissue alone causes no change in sexual behavior. But destroying the vomeronasal nerve alone prevents mating and copulation in a full third of the tested animals—proof of the intimate but apparently not exclusive connection between the vomeronasal system and sexual behavior.

Rats, too, exhibit strong associations between sexual/reproductive behavior and the vomeronasal system. As noted earlier in the chapter, a relationship has been found between male rat odors and the development of the female rat reproductive systems. Perhaps more significantly, once a female rat has been impregnated, she will abort the fetus if she comes into contact with the urine of a different male—other than the one that impregnated her. If, on the other hand, the nerves leading from the vomeronasal organ are cut after she has been impregnated, the female rat can complete her pregnancy even if she contacts urine from other males.

Experiments done with voles, small mouselike creatures, further underline the vomeronasal/reproductive connection. It has traditionally been assumed that the ovulation cycles of most mammalian species are regulated by biological rhythms governing release of certain ovulation-inducing hormones. However, it has been found that in voles, at least, male pheromones play a significant role in inducing the ovulation cycle. In one experiment, a drop of adult male vole urine was placed on the lip of an adult female. When the female was examined after the passage of as little as one hour, her accessory olfactory bulb showed a significant increase in the levels of two hormones considered essential in the mechanism by which ovulation takes place, indicating that it is the detection of male vole pheromones by the female vole's vomeronasal system that stimulates the production of those hormones.

Research is also underway with animals to investigate the exact nature of how the vomeronasal system works. In one experiment, researchers allowed male guinea pigs to sniff at female guinea pig urine mixed with molecules of a dye that fluoresces under ultraviolet light. When, after a brief period, they examined sections of the male's vomeronasal organ under ultraviolet light, they found it glowed brightly with molecules of the dye that had been absorbed with the female urine and made their way to the vomeronasal organ. Thus, research has well documented the existence of the vomeronasal system in many of the lower species.

But what about *humans?* Do we have a vomeronasal system— another sense of smell that perceives certain chemical signals in the world around us and transforms them into bodily responses so prim-

itive that they are completely unconscious? Do we, in fact, maintain
a deeply rooted, physiological connection between certain scents and
various types of social interaction, including sexuality? In other
words, can we detect human pheromones?

Slowly evidence is coming together showing that *some* humans
may indeed have working vomeronasal organs. As we mentioned in
Chapter 4, it has been established that all human fetuses start out
with a vomeronasal system. As is the case with the presence of gills
during early stages of fetal development, the vomeronasal system, a
relic of our reptilian past, is part of the very developmental process
by which the individual comes about. But whereas gills disappear
during the fetus's first few months, the vomeronasal organ remains,
perhaps persisting in a still undetermined percentage of the adult
population. (It may be the memories this sensory system recorded
when we were young which are suddenly stimulated in later life and
manifest themselves as the déjà vu experience described earlier.)

Unfortunately only an autopsy (or very expensive CAT scans) can
prove whether or not a given individual has a vomeronasal organ
with a set of nerves running back to the brain, and no way has yet
been found to show once and for all whether even if a vomeronasal
system is present in humans, it actually functions. The kind of
conclusive proof obtained in experiments on animals with severed
vomeronasal nerve pathways is obviously impossible to obtain with
humans. But researchers at the Monell Chemical Senses Center are
making considerable headway with findings about the use of human
pheromones. They have shown, for instance, that the composition
of certain odors in vaginal secretions fluctuates with the menstrual
cycle. Lactic acid, for instance, is higher when a woman is most
fertile, which may help explain why men find the odor of vaginal
secretions "less intense" and "less unpleasant" around the time of
ovulation.

Levels of sulfur in a woman's breath also fluctuate with the menstrual cycle, increasing during menstruation, accounting for what
some women call "menses breath"; perhaps this has evolved to make
copulation a little less pleasant during this nonfertile time. So reli-
able are these cycles of chemical activity that it may actually be

possible to develop a "fertile period" test based on the chemical composition of a woman's breath. And these same chemicals may account for the ability of many men to recognize a breath sample of the opposite sex on the basis of smell alone. (Women, using a still undiscovered component in men's breath, do even better at this kind of sex identification, with some women able to tell if a breath sample comes from a male with 95 percent accuracy.)

The chemical signals produced by males are mostly derived from male androgen hormones which are secreted by the male testes, although androgens are present to a lesser extent in women where they are secreted by the gonads. As the ad claims, it is true both that men perspire more and that their underarm odor is more intense; this is because androgens are secreted through the sweat glands where they are given their characteristic odor by bacteria that live in the armpits. Androstenone and its derivative alpha androstenol, androgens which are the musky, perfume-like components of sweat, are quite different from the component of sweat that produces its unpleasant, acrid odor. (This unpleasant smell seems to increase with fear and nervousness, accounting perhaps for "the smell of fear" and the problem many experience with "nervous perspiration" mentioned earlier.)

Androgens may affect behavior, especially that associated with sexuality. In one experiment, women wearing masks containing androstenol responded to assertive male job applicants more favorably. In another experiment, women felt more attracted to men whose clothing had been treated with the substance. Other studies show women's reactions to photographs of male strangers to be more positive when a small amount of androstenol is secretly sprayed into the air or when wearing masks containing it. In still another experiment, when androstenone was sprayed onto a chair in a waiting room that was not normally used by women, they often chose to sit in it; men tended to avoid it after it was sprayed.

A woman's receptivity to androstenone becomes significantly sharper during ovulation, perhaps enabling her to be more easily "turned on" by a male giving off this signal. Androstenone also figures prominently into the reproductive activities of swine. When a sow is fertile, her sensitivity to the chemicals in boar secretions appears to increase naturally, making her better able to sense the boar's androstenol and androstenone; these substances, in turn, make her more receptive to his advances. Interestingly, the same substance has also been found, by German researchers at the Technical University of Munich and the Lubeck School of Medicine, in the subterranean truffle fungi, considered such an epicurean delight. Truffles grow as deep as three feet underground, and the main way of locating them is to bring a sow out into the field who will not only sniff the ground until the truffle is located, but then dig into the ground after it with passionate intensity. The mushroom contains some two times the amount of androstenol as is found in the male pig's blood, where it is secreted by the testes. It is no wonder the sow's efforts are so fierce. And this chemical may perhaps even account for why humans find the truffle to be such a delicacy.

The most significant pheromonal research to date, however, is still underway at the Monell Chemical Senses Center, where scientists are attempting to duplicate on humans the experiments linking pheromones with the reproductive cycle previously noted in hamsters, rats, and voles.

It is already known, for instance, that female odors bring about a synchrony in other females' menstrual cycles, so that women who live together often end up with the same menstrual cycle timing. New research, however, is attempting to show that male odors are also vital in the regular functioning of a woman's cycle, related to the observation that women with irregular periods are often those who are not having regular sex. The hypothesis is that these women are irregular because of lack of exposure to male odors. One experiment involves putting male-odor-containing substances on a gauze pad on the women's upper lips. If any change is noted in the regularity of their periods, it will help to show that pheromones are involved in regulating female sexuality just as they are involved in the reproductive cycles of other species. The results of the experiment are not yet known.

As for the other side of the picture—the influence women have on men—we have already noted the fluctuations in the composition of female breath and vaginal secretions that make them less unpleasant during times when copulation is ideal. But females also actively attract males with their pheromones. In rhesus monkeys it has been shown that when the female monkey is fertile, she secretes certain fatty acids known collectively as copulin in her vaginal secretions, and this substance affects male sexual behavior. The same substance has been isolated in human vaginal secretions, and an experiment has shown that smearing this substance on a woman's body can increase male arousal and desire. As for why these experiments only work some of the time, the answer may be simply that the substance only affects those males with working vomeronasal systems.

Humans have, of course, progressed beyond the stage when presumably, like dogs, we sniffed when we met another individual rather than shaking hands. But the same chemical signals that we sniffed for then are probably still at work, supplementing the myriad conscious and unconscious signals and gestures that come into play when we meet. It is ironic that so much money is spent covering up body odors with perfumes that promise greater sexual attraction when the body's own chemistry is the greatest sexual attractant known.

Chapter Eight
Illusion and Reality

By this time she had found her way into a tidy little room with a table in the window, and on it (as she had hoped) a fan and two or three pairs of tiny white kid gloves: she took up the fan and a pair of the gloves, and was just going to leave the room, when her eyes fell upon a tiny bottle that stood near the looking-glass. There was no label this time with the words "DRINK ME." But nevertheless she uncorked it and put it to her lips. "I know *something* is sure to happen," she said to herself, "whenever I eat or drink anything; so I'll just see what this bottle does."

Lewis Carroll, ALICE IN WONDERLAND

Hallucinations, nightmares, ecstatic visions, delirium tremens, dreams, migraine attacks, drug and alcohol intoxication, insulin shock, delirium of fevers, epilepsy, psychotic episodes. The world of illusion and the world of reality, one perceived by the mind and the other by the senses, one a mere figment of the imagination and the other a true reckoning of the essential plan of the cosmos, one to be mistrusted as belonging to the dark, hidden part of the soul and the other connected with the bright light of reason.

The illusion that the human species can somehow cross the boundaries between illusion and reality (using logic and reason to understand irrational instincts and expecting that mystical revelations will reveal the reality of the physical universe) is perhaps as old as consciousness itself. The duality is often expressed as a conflict

between science and religion. In earlier days, when religion was the
dominant force and science was just emerging, the conflict between
the known and the unknowable, the seen and the unseen, was
simply expressed: whatever could be perceived with the senses,
whatever corresponded to the current notion of reality, whatever
pleased the current aesthetic was, by definition, created by God and
therefore good. Whatever, on the other hand, did not fit a logical
sense of order—all kinds of "magick," necromancy, trickery, sor-
cery, and so forth—was evil, and could not be explained by the
laws of science. Science, the servant of God's greater glory, could
be used only to explain the beauty of his good works.

For example, even the simple sleight-of-hand act, subject of considerable enthrallment and wonder, was plainly a manifestation of
evil since it apparently did not obey "natural" laws. Those who
performed the magick were considered villainous sorcerers. Today,
however, with science grown to equal religion in stature, we explain
the sleight-of-hand trick as the result of a simple phenomenon: the
magician's hand moves faster than the observer can perceive it.

A similar illusion allows us to perceive movies and television as
smooth, continuous motion rather than as a series of separate
frames. The eye and the brain mechanisms that interpret the perception can register a new image every twentieth of a second. But when
pictures are changed more quickly than that, as is the case with a
motion picture projector or the television system, the "memory" of
one frame is still present when the next one comes along, so one
blends into the other. The brain, like a computer, averages the two
images and creates a smooth transition between them, even though
the projector has actually shown one frame, advanced to the next
image, and shown that one too, literally faster than the eye can see.

But is the sleight-of-hand trick any less fascinating today in light
of the new scientific explanation of how it works, or are moving
pictures any less believable once we realize they are caused by an
illusion of motion? For although we *know* the magician is moving
his hand extremely quickly, we cannot actually *see* it. The result is
that the simple illusion opens up a corner of the mind that somehow
wants to believe in magic and exercise a simple act of faith. It may

be contrary to rational scientific explanation, but we believe the coin disappears.

In fact, the dual nature of scientific and religious consciousness has never actually been bridged, despite the growth of modern science to encompass virtually every aspect of the world as we know it. Some things are by their very nature a mystery, and, by definition, not understandable except by belief. And even if there is some "ultimate truth to the universe," we are prevented from understanding it for exactly the same reasons that we want to understand it in the first place. The same psychic tendency that creates gods and religions to explain the "larger forces" at work in the universe keeps transforming the "ultimate reality" into a less and less knowable energy which cannot—indeed *must* not—be understood.

Even if we had the emotional apparatus that would allow us to experience ultimate reality, however, a far more concrete obstacle stands between us and the mystical vision of god and cosmos: the physical apparatus of our far-from-perfect sensory systems would probably not allow us to see it, even if it were literally staring us in the face. Humans, it turns out, are not perfect physical specimens in total harmony with nature and able to perceive it in its entirety.

Humans perceive what can only be described as a minuscule portion of the continuum of nature, and even that portion is not as detailed or "continuous" as reality itself. In the case of light, for example, we are not nearly as sensitive to some colors within the "visible" spectrum as others and have no visual sensory organs for ultraviolet or infrared light at all.

"Ultimate truth," it might be observed, may simply be what lies outside our rather limited ability to perceive the universe. And the fantasy writer's "parallel world"—existing alongside the one we can see but moving much too fast for our eyes to be sensitive to it— makes conceptual if not rational, observable sense. Is this, one might seriously ask, where the coin goes when the magician makes it disappear?

The imperfection of the senses confronts us at every turn—even in the portion of the spectrum we *can* perceive. Every sense has its weakness (the speed limit of vision that permits the sleight-of-hand trick and the illusion of motion, for example), and virtually no experience can be reported without the bias of the sensory system contributing heavily to the data. If you taste a glass of ordinary water, then a glass of soda water, both at the same temperature, the carbonated water will taste colder. Similarly, intense freezing sensations—such as those encountered when the skin touches dry ice —sometimes give the illusion of burning.

Optical illusions are by far the most common of the many "misrepresentations" made by the senses. Most familiar are such patterns as the two lines of absolutely equal length, one with arrow-like points and the other with outward-projecting lines, which appear to be strikingly unequal. In another familiar example, perfectly parallel lines can be made to appear bowed when placed alongside other, curved figures.

What makes illusions so intriguing is that when one studies the "reality," it's obvious that the two lines are of equal length or straight; but, as in the sleight-of-hand trick, the measured, "scientific" data directly conflict with the supposedly observed phenomena.

These simple confusions between illusion and reality are not that significant in themselves, of course, except in that they reveal some major gaps in human sensory apparatus. They lead, however, to an extremely important question about the nature of all human consciousness. How much of what is perceived in nature as reality, we must ask, can be trusted as "real"? How many supposedly "true," "scientific" phenomena of nature are merely illusions reported by the senses to the brain, which simply accepts them without question?

"The earth is at the center of the universe," one might have asserted at one time, noting with absolute certainty that the sun and all the planets and stars rotate around us. "The leaves of the tree are green," we insist with equal fervor. The senses, of course, report that color is as much "a property of things" as their hardness and softness, something which must surely pervade every atom and molecule of the substance. On the contrary, the property of color occurs only at the very outermost layer of molecules on the surface how the viewer is oriented. If you tape a square of paper to the wall, then view it with your head turned on its side, the square will continue to appear as a square and not a diamond, even though if the paper itself were rotated to the same degree the perception would change. On the other hand, since the visual system normally assigns "up" and "down" based on an object's position within the environment (we "know" that the top of the piece of paper faces the top of the wall), the senses can be fooled into falsely assigning "top" and "bottom" if the environment is distorted. If the image of the room and the wall are tilted 45 degrees, the piece of paper taped to the wall will appear to be a diamond even though it would normally be seen as a square.

The other theory of visual modeling advocated by Gestalt psychology takes the view that, rather than a simple information processing system such as described above, the organizing process in the brain is based on more "human" concerns. In this understanding, one of the most powerful organizing principles is "simplicity." A favorite example is the open cube shape that can be drawn using nine intersecting lines. The lines, of course, are only two-dimensional, and the information received by the cells of the retina is also only two-dimensional. But when viewed, the figure is almost always interpreted as a cube despite the literally hundreds of other possible interpretations of the lines and angles. Gestalt pattern theory suggests that the cube is seen because it represents the simplest, most logical way of organizing the data. In the cube shape, all the angles are 90 degrees, all the lines are of equal length, and all the pieces fit neatly into a coherent form.

The Gestalt notion of modeling is used to explain another major kind of visual illusion—the ambiguous figure or the reversible figure (illustrated in Chapter 6), in which the viewer can see two interpretations of the same image. In these situations, the perceptual process in the brain literally switches back and forth between two equally plausible interpretations of the same sensory data. The switchover is completely unconscious (though one can force the mind to hold on to one of the ambiguous interpretations for a while before switching back to the other), and reflects a basic feature of the perceptual process itself.

of an object. Light falls on the object's surface molecules, cau
them to vibrate. While most of this energy is absorbed and t
formed into heat by the internal molecular structure, molecul
the surface of the object become excited, then re-radiate light
particular electromagnetic frequency (color). So not only is the
ject not composed of colored substances, as the senses tend to re
(without light the object would be totally colorless), but it doe
even "reflect light of different colors falling on it," as an ea
theory once explained it. The human sense of color actually rep
data on the most superficial process of a vastly complex phys
universe, reflecting more our own need to distinguish objects
backgrounds than it does any essential feature of how the univ
is organized.

In a sense, every piece of sensory data that comes into the br
is organized by perceptual processes that enable the information
be used—processes and models that do not distinguish betwe
"reality" and its organization into patterns recognizable by t
human brain. The exact nature of these models, however, has be
the cause of considerable scientific controversy in recent years. (
the one hand, one group of psychologists postulate a set of "learn
visual experiences" to which all incoming data is compared. Th
other principal theory suggests a set of "information processin
devices" in the brain, rather like the data processing found in
computer, which filter data according to a more precise, probabl
innate modeling process that does not depend on learned visua
patterning.

The latter group cites as an example the apparently universal
assignment of "top" and "bottom," "left" and "right," "front" and
"back" which we discussed in Chapter 4 in connection with the
development of a child's visual system. This theory of modeling
cites as one of its clearest examples the figures of a diamond and a
square (see illustration in Chapter 6), which are identical except
that one is rotated 45 degrees. But the square is seen as a square
and the diamond as a diamond, and the two are not seen to be
simple transformations of one another.

The square/diamond differentiation is not simply a function of

One of the clearest examples of this kind of ambiguity is situations in which one cannot tell the difference between the foreground and the background—the scientific explanation of the artistry of M. C. Escher (whose work is illustrated in Chapter 6). The use of light and dark figures, both recognizable, in Escher's prints makes it impossible to tell whether a work depicts white figures on a dark background or dark figures on a white background (see, for example, Angels and Devils, shown on page 140).

A similar background/foreground situation occurs with the face/vase figure shown on page 119, in which one sees either two dark faces silhouetted against a light background or a light vase against a dark background.

But it is not necessary that the forms be recognizable. Escher's work and the face/vase figure are based on a seemingly universal observation; but any wavy line drawn through a circle illustrates the point. See, for example, Divided Circle, page 136. The line is seen as the edge of a wave-like contour in the foreground of the image that covers part of the circle which is seen to be in the background. But is the "wave" coming from the right or the left, and is it covering the right or the left half of the background circle? The foreground "wave" cannot be both at the same time; our perceptual process insists on defining it as one or the other.

The same phenomenon operates with jigsaw puzzle pieces. The line defining the "in" piece actually is identical in shape to the line defining the "out" piece. But it takes a somewhat special skill to be able to match the two lines into a single piece.

Ambiguous perceptions can occur in three-dimensional situations as well. If you take a white index card, fold it lengthwise down the middle, place it on a table illuminated from the side, and view it from the top, you will perceive a roof-like shape. After staring at it for a few moments, however, the shape appears to reverse and you will find yourself looking at a form more like an open book. Without any change in the physical reality, the brain has profoundly changed the way it orders the data. This is because two ways of organizing the data are equally "simple" and valid, and first one, then the other, is being used to order the information being reported.

Even more significant than the brain's shifting back and forth between interpretations, however, is that as it shifts interpretive models to explain the shape it creates a set of visual data that conform to what it thinks it ought to be seeing—not to what is actually seen by the eyes. Thus, as it transforms the "roof" into a "book," the brain assumes that the part of the form it now perceives as hidden in the new orientation *should* be reflecting less light; it obliges by seeing that part of the form as gray and shaded, while the portion that should be reflecting more light is seen to be almost glowing. But absolutely no change has taken place in nature— merely in our perception of it.

What, then, makes any one particular interpretation of data more valid than another? In most cases, simply the general agreement that one interpretation is "real" because most people experience it that way. As we will see later in this discussion, hallucinations can be shown to represent not something that is completely "unreal" but merely something experienced in other than the normal, or usual, manner. The same can be said of dreams—and of drug-related experiences. For the person who has taken a psychotropic substance, the experience of "a separate reality" is as convincing as the voices of the saints must have been for Joan of Arc. Witness this description by Carlos Castaneda of his first experience with mescaline:

> The water looked strangely shiny, glossy, like a thick varnish. I wanted to ask don Juan about it and laboriously I tried to voice my thoughts in English, but then I realized he did not speak English. I experienced a very confusing moment, and became aware of the fact that although there was a clear thought in my mind, I could not speak. I wanted to comment on the strange quality of the water, but what followed next was not speech; it was the feeling of my unvoiced thoughts coming out of my mouth in a sort of liquid form. It was an effortless sensation of vomiting without the contractions of the diaphragm. It was a pleasant flow of liquid words.
>
> I drank. And the feeling that I was vomiting disappeared. By that time all noises had vanished and I found I had difficulty focusing my eyes. I looked for don Juan and as I turned my head I noticed that

my field of vision had diminished to a circular area in front of my eyes. This feeling was neither frightening nor discomforting, but, quite to the contrary, it was a novelty; I could literally sweep the ground by focusing on one spot and then moving my head slowly in any direction. . . .

I saw the juncture of the porch floor and the wall. I turned my head slowly to the right, following the wall, and saw don Juan sitting against it. I shifted my head to the left in order to focus on the water. I found the bottom of the pan; I raised my head slightly and saw a medium-size black dog approaching. I saw him coming toward the water. The dog began to drink. I raised my hand to push him away from my water; I focused my pinpoint vision on the dog to carry on the movement, and suddenly I saw him become transparent. The water was a shiny, viscous liquid. I saw it going down the dog's throat into his body. I saw it flowing evenly through his entire length and then shooting out through each one of the hairs. I saw the iridescent fluid traveling along the length of each individual hair and then projecting out of the hairs to form a long, white, silky mane.

His sensory input distorted by the drug, Castaneda actually sees a different world than normal—and this vision becomes the basis for a different reality. Is each individual's reality, then, as different as individual variations in vision and visual acuity? Don Juan suggests that any of us can learn the tricks necessary to distort vision and therefore to enter the separate reality which the brain creates to explain the new vision.

Returning to our original question, how much of what we perceive as reality is actually an illusion? The answer currently provided by modern psychology is "virtually everything." Not only is perception itself a highly subjective experience, but many principles based on perception can also be interpreted simply as a convenient way of describing what may actually be unknowable after all. The sun does not revolve around the earth even though the senses may see it that way. Color is not an inherent property of things but merely the way the eye perceives radiation reflected from their surfaces. And many of the scientific explanations concerning the operation of the universe are probably human conveniences based on our somewhat limited abilities of perception.

Indeed, the grandest illusion of all may be the most basic scientific principle—that no two objects may occupy the same space at the same time. The statement is based, of course, on a practically universal perception of the processes of the physical universe. But is this any more valid than the perception that the sun moves around the earth?

Actually, the principle that two objects cannot occupy the same space at the same time can be seen as an extension of a profound weakness of human perception: an object cannot be part of two patterns at the same time. Presented with a set of ambiguous data —simple square tiles on a bathroom floor, as illustrated in Chapter 6, for example—the brain organizes them into discrete patterns. After a few minutes of staring, another pattern will be present, with the brain's perceptual process having shifted gears and switched to an alternative organization plan. In a few minutes more, still another pattern may be seen, or the first pattern may reappear. But even after almost tormenting struggle, it is virtually impossible to hold more than one plan of organization in the mind at once.

The same factors can be seen at work in an experiment in which four light bulbs are arranged in a square on a flat piece of board (clockwise A, B, C, D), then flashed in patterns to experimental observers. When bulbs at the diagonal corners are flashed alternately (A + C, then B + D), the illusion of motion is created as in a theater marquee. The motion is seen as either horizontal (A moves to B while C moves to D, and then back again) or vertical (A moves to D while B moves to C, then back again). After staring at the pattern for a few minutes, however, the observers almost always reported that the direction they had first perceived had changed to the other. So complete was the change that the observers almost always assumed that it was the bulb positions that had been altered or the electronic circuits retimed. As in the reversible figure examples, however, the only change was in the perceptual patterns of the observers' brains.

The brain, in this case at least, orders the nature of physical reality rather than objectively perceiving it. In yet another example, if you look at a field of regularly spaced dots, your brain will organize it into either vertical or horizontal patterns. As you stare at the dots, their arrangement will appear to change from one to the other. But the two can never coexist.

But if we humans are incapable of perceiving objects in two patterns at the same time, can we make the assumption that nature itself is organized the same way? There is at least some possibility that the fundamental law of physics is merely human convenience after all—that two objects may, indeed, occupy the same space at the same time, although we cannot see them.

This, at any rate, was part of the philosophy of Castaneda's main character Don Juan, a Yaqui Indian sorcerer/medicine man who based many of his teachings on his ability to truly "see" things, rather than simply observing them as a passive spectator. This "act of seeing," common to many spiritual people, may in fact represent an ability to break down the Gestalt of the ordinary world and see things in patterns different from those of normal perception, setting the mind off balance and allowing for all sorts of cognitive and perceptual processes not normally possible—including the perception of the kind of multiple-leveled patterning that allows more than one object to occupy the same space at the same time.

Once the barriers defining normal perception have been broken down, in fact, it becomes possible to perceive and experience all manner of unusual phenomena—or the same phenomena as usual, but in a different way. The difference can be as profound as rotating the square of paper until the point where it is no longer a square but a diamond!

This breaking down process appears to relate directly to the physiological processes that constitute memory—as we shall see shortly. Interfering with the chemical processes of the brain, therefore, becomes a prime method of inducing this kind of vision, evident in Castaneda's experience with mescaline and also common in religious ceremonies throughout the world. It has particular importance to shamanism, where the "medicine man" has a specific interest in opening himself up to visual and aural possibilities, and in breaking down ordinary reality in order to literally "see" the future or the course of action the group should take, or the cause of an illness and its cure. The shaman opens himself to these experiences by deliberately breaking down the barriers between himself and the rest of nature. Consider, for example, this account of Yakut (Eskimo) Indians at the turn of the century from a contemporary account by W. Sieroszewski analyzed in Mircea Eliade's *Shamanism: Archaic Techniques of Ecstasy:*

"The shaman stares into the fire on the hearth; he yawns, hiccups spasmodically, from time to time he is shaken by nervous tremors. He puts on his shamanic costume and begins to smoke. Soon afterward his face grows pale, his head falls on his breast, his eyes half close. A white mare's hide is spread in the middle of the yurt. The shaman drinks cold water and genuflects to the four cardinal points, spitting water to right and left. Silence reigns in the yurt. The shaman's assistant throws some horse hairs in the fire, then covers it over completely with ashes. The darkness now becomes total. The shaman sits down on the mare's hide and dreams, facing south. All hold their breath.

"Suddenly a succession of shrill cries, piercing as the screech of steel, sounds from no-one knows where; then all is silent again. Another cry; and now from above, now from below, now before, now behind the shaman rise mysterious sounds: nervous, terrifying yawns, hysterical hiccups; it is as if one heard the plaintive cry of the lapwing mingled with the crowing of a falcon and interrupted by the whistling of the woodcock; it is the shaman making these sounds but changing the tone of his voice.

"Suddenly he stops; again silence reigns, except for a faint humming, like that of a mosquito. The shaman begins to beat his drum. He murmurs a song. The song and the drumming rise in crescendo. Soon the shaman is bellowing. . . .

"On the arrival of the amagat [spirit, inspiration] the shaman begins leaping, makes swift, violent gestures. Finally he takes his place in the center of the yurt, the fire is rekindled, and he begins to drum and dance again. He flings himself into the air, sometimes as high as four feet. He cries out wildly. This is followed by another pause; then in a low, serious voice he intones a silent hymn. . . ."

We must note again here that the Yakut shaman's power and prestige derive exclusively from his capacity for ecstasy. . . . It is still to his mystical capacities that the shaman owes his ability to discover and combat the evil spirits that have seized the patient's soul: he does not confine himself to exorcising them, he takes them into his own body, "possesses" them, tortures and expels them. All this is because he shares their nature, that is, he is free to leave his body, to transport himself to great distances, to descend to the underworld, to scale the sky, and so on.

The shaman, in other words, is one who specializes—either through the use of psychotropic, mind-altering drugs or else through a self-induced state of ecstatic vision—in taking leave of his ordinary senses, in becoming seemingly blind and deaf to the ordinary world in his trance-like state, in order to perceive and ultimately enter the "other world," the mystical realm that lies outside ordinary experience (and inside the shaman's own imaginings). And, because he himself appears so different, does things so differently from ordinary men, he carries those witnessing his strange behavior along with him into the trance, forcing them to break the mold of everyday visual experience.

An account of a more modern shamanistic experience is provided by Sam Boone, a 65-year-old Navajo Indian who is a member of the peyote-based Native American Church:

> When someone has called a meeting, first they roll up a cigarette [a mixture of tobacco and other herbs], and then everyone prays with it. And then they smoke it and then they put it against the crescent [a religious emblem drawn on the floor]—the rope man [leader of the ceremony] puts his cigarette against the crescent and then people on either side do it too. After that, they pass the sage around. And everyone smells it and puts it on themselves.
>
> After that, they pass the medicine [peyote buttons] around to eat —chopped up any way. And then the rope man prays for whoever called the meeting. And then after that they sing the starting song, until about 11:30 [P.M.] Then the midnight water call, when they blow a whistle four times and on the third time the fire chief brings

in the water and then he sets it down real carefully, because the
water and fire are real precious things. You could stay alive by water
and fire. But they can also damage you, too. After that the rope man
prays. . . .

I got into the medicine about twenty-five years ago. I met this
boy where we were working and he said he was going to take me to
the reservation to a meeting. The next morning when I got out, I
saw San Francisco peak. I could see everything that was on that peak
—bushes and trees and yucca plants . . . it was like a picture, really
close. So I figured to myself that I must have taken something really
terrible . . . worse than drinking. I was really high. So I went out
and dug a hole and crawled into it . . . I was crying.

After we had finished eating breakfast, I wanted to take off home.
I started driving my truck, a '64 Ford, kind of old. But when I
started driving fast, it seemed like everything was going to fall apart.
I came back at ten o'clock that night, barely crawling. That medicine
is really powerful.

At another meeting, it [the peyote] showed me a boat. The boat
was going and I saw one man standing there in a kind of fog. And
when I looked closely, it was me. That was right before I went
overseas with the army.

The next meeting I went to it was at Christmas. The medicine
showed me the United States flag when I got out in the morning. It
showed me the bright flag—it was really waving—it was as big as
this house.

I decided to go into the meeting one more time, and it showed
me what I had done wrong. The medicine is there to help me see
what I have done. It showed me an eagle. When I looked through
the porthole of the hogan [meeting house], I saw an eagle flying by.
And then it set wing over a big tree. Then he became mad and came
down and was going to hit me with its big talons. But I didn't get
scared. And he turned back into a silver dollar again.

After that, the peyote showed me the world with three circles of
cars around it. I figured to myself, "Some day I'm going to have
cars." And then it showed me a silver dollar and I figured, "Some
day I'm going to have money."

The things I see during a meeting are very real for me. It's just
like church—you've got to believe. If you see it . . . if it shows you,
you've got to believe it.

Shamans and medicine men, of course, aren't the only group that "takes leave of its senses" on a regular basis. Schizophrenics and others who are mentally ill are also "out of their minds," and often demonstrate the same kinds of physical manifestations as the shaman. Schizophrenics, too, often have a view of reality in which familiar patterns are distorted so that the patient sees a completely different world order—one that may be as threatening as it is beneficial.

By this point it should be evident that the realm of mystery and illusion is far from simple chicanery. Whether the result of an optical illusion, or a drug-related experience, or a natural chemical imbalance, illusion is simply another way of seeing and experiencing the same world that is seen through ordinary perception. And it is in this context that science has made its most important discovery about illusion: dreams, hallucinations, ecstatic experiences, and the like may actually be a way of representing another world parallel to that seen by conscious perception—a world "seen" by unconscious perception.

This parallel world cannot be dismissed as the figment of a science fantasy writer's imagination (though imagination is one of the primary ways this world has of expressing itself). Nor are unconscious perceptions "seen" only by those with a special gift—the perceptions exist in everyone, though some put up barriers to experiencing them. This parallel world is the world of the unconscious mind, and connected to it is a well-developed system of hidden senses.

The idea of a parallel world of unconscious mind is not mystical imagining but hard scientific fact, although rational explanations are not always the best way to describe how the unconscious works. According to the new model, any data coming in from the senses apparently go through two separate thought processes. One is more developed, conscious, rational—a "thought-forming" process. Simultaneously, however, the other, unconscious, more "primitive" process is acting on much the same information, storing it in a more personal memory in which objects and events are linked not by a logical syntax but by individual association. Conscious and uncon-

scious thus constantly provide two often different views of "reality,"
neither one, in fact, more valid than the other.

The world of the shaman is the world of his own unconscious—
and that of the audience whose conscious thought is thrown aside
by the powerful magic the shaman uses to direct messages at the
audience's unconscious. The same might be said of art—that it sets
conscious communication aside and speaks directly to the unconscious. It doesn't take a shaman or an artist, though, to reveal this
inner, unconscious working. Ordinary dreaming makes use of an
almost identical thought process.

Like many things associated with the unconscious, it has only
been within the past century that the dream has even been understood as a "human" phenomenon and not something placed in the
mind by evil or beneficent spirits (depending on the dream's content). The breakthrough in understanding was, of course, the work
of Sigmund Freud, who finally presented a picture of dreams and
dreaming that could be understood logically, in scientific terms,
rather than as disorganized, chaotic, and therefore somehow wrong.
Said another pioneering psychologist, Carl Jung:

> It is regrettable that in this year of grace 1931, more than half a
> century since Carus formulated the concept of the unconscious, over
> a century since Kant spoke of the "immeasurable . . . field of ob-
> scure ideas" and nearly two hundred years since Leibniz postulated
> an unconscious psychic activity, not to mention the achievements of
> Janet, Flournoy and Freud—that after all this, the actuality of the
> unconscious should still be a matter for controversy. . . . It is ob-
> vious that dream-analysis stands or falls with this hypothesis. With-
> out it the dream appears to be merely a freak of nature, a meaningless
> conglomerate of memory-fragments left over from the happenings of
> the day.

It was, of course, the great psychologists such as Freud and Jung
who first described the uniquely personal nature of dream visions,
linking them to psychic processes and likening dreams to *"image-
ination"* in their highly creative, expressive reworking of everyday

events. Jung took the process even further, saying that many dream images proceed from an area of the psyche that may never have seen or experienced things directly, but that contains a collective unconscious which is inherited by members of the species just as are our upright posture and moveable thumb. How else, Jung asked, could such widely diverse cultures and people, including modern men and women who had had no contact with the ancient images, evolve such similar patterns and shapes as the mandala?

No discussion of dreaming, of course, can proceed without an understanding of sleep itself, and in this area science made some major discoveries in the 1950s and 1960s. It had been previously assumed that sleep was simply a lack of wakefulness—that the brain, no longer stimulated by features of the environment, simply stopped transmitting the signals that constituted wakefulness. At the same time, sleep was seen as a good opportunity for rest and relaxation of tired muscles and organs. As Jung and Freud had predicted, however, with their notions of "an undiscovered part of the self" that partly revealed itself in dreams, sleep was shown to be a regular, necessary part of living—a state of being that had its own very specific physiology and was far more than being simply "not awake."

The key to this understanding is the almost clockwork-like regularity of sleep cycles, five to seven a night depending on the length of time one sleeps. The process begins almost as soon as the eyes are closed and the brain's electrical activity begins to transform itself from the mostly irregular, unsynchronized activity that characterizes waking to the slow, rhythmic, synchronized activity that characterizes sleep. Within thirty to forty-five minutes of falling asleep, the brain has passed through Levels I, II, and III and enters deep, Level IV, sleep—in which the sleeper is almost impossible to arouse, breathing, heartbeat, and blood pressure are slow and highly regular, skeletal muscles are completely relaxed except for changes in sleeping position which occur every five to twenty minutes, but gastrointestinal activity is fairly high. To distinguish it from other stages, this type of sleep is referred to as NREM, or non-rapid-eye-movement sleep.

Dreams during NREM sleep are of two profoundly different types. One, rarely remembered, consists of somewhat conscious, often pleasant, but not generally emotionally involving thoughts. The second, vividly remembered, is the classical nightmare (as opposed to the "bad dreams" of REM sleep). Though so sharply, personally experienced, the nightmare has some fairly universal symptoms, including an intense anxiety with a characteristic sweating, dilated pupils, and rapid heartbeat. The nightmare is almost always a physical sensation—a shortness of breath, a paralysis, as if something were sitting on the chest. Often nightmare victims report an intense, life-or-death struggle to break free of the restriction —a true fight for life against the possessing demon. Interestingly, mythology associates nightmares with the term *incubus,* whose Latin root means "to lie upon" but which also signifies the demon of Medieval legends which was said to visit the sleeper (usually a woman) and plant within her the devil's seed.

The same phenomenon accounts for children's night terrors—in which the child wakes up screaming, usually some thirty minutes after going to bed and during Level III or IV sleep. Still another deep-sleep phenomenon is somnambulism, or sleepwalking, again with characteristic physical activity but with little recall on the part of the sleepwalker.

Interestingly, one's need for deep, Level IV sleep decreases markedly with age, so that the nightmares of younger children occur less frequently in adults simply because adults spend less time in the sleep stage in which nightmares occur.

After a few minutes in Level IV, the process is reversed and the sleeper slowly rises through Levels III and II to Level I again, the rhythmic brain cycles becoming more and more frequent. At Level I the brain wave cycles are quite frequent, and the sleeper can be easily awakened.

However, it's not until one full ninety-minute cycle of falling to Level IV and rising to Level I that real "dreaming" takes place, accompanied by profound physiological changes. Suddenly the heartbeat and blood pressure increase, breathing becomes more irregular, brain activity is no longer synchronized in waves, and gastrointestinal activity ceases. More important, there is a radical loss of muscle tone while the head and neck muscles are prevented from moving. Simultaneously, the eyes begin moving about and the muscles of the middle ear begin contracting; REM (rapid eye movement) sleep has been achieved, and the sleeper is dreaming. Though difficult to arouse by external stimuli, the dreamer often wakes spontaneously.

Everybody experiences REM sleep, and everybody dreams several times a night, depending on the number of REM cycles experienced —except for those deliberately deprived of sleep, and alcoholics, who spend their sleeping hours in the stupor of Level IV sleep (for them, the lack of dream images is substituted for by real-life hallucinations). And as the night progresses, the dream content of the REM periods becomes more and more intense—marked physiologically by more intense brain and eye movement activity. If the sleeper is wakened within eight minutes of a REM period, the dream can almost always be remembered. But since the most intense dreams occur at the end of a night's sleep, and since one often wakes in the morning just following a REM period, it is often the morning dream that is remembered. Since Level IV sleep occurs primarily during the first part of the night's sleep, and since REM periods become more and more frequent and last longer and longer as the night progresses, REM activity occupies nearly a quarter of an average night's sleep, deep sleep (Level IV) about 15 percent, and Level II about 50 percent.

The physiological understanding of the sleep/dreaming process, however, is only part of the brand-new picture science is creating. Perhaps more significant is a truly fundamental explanation of the origin of dream images as arising within the same, distinct part of the brain in which the imaginative, "magical" perceptual process resides. What was once thought to be the realm of demons and evil spirits has been shown to be an understandable "human" process after all, just as the sleight-of-hand trick can now be understood as no longer belonging to the spirit world.

What makes dream images so different from ordinary perception, so unusual, so startling, of course, is not that they are so totally different after all. In fact, since the dreamer (and not some outside force) is doing all the dreaming, the dream image must necessarily belong to some aspect of reality the dreamer has experienced, unless one accepts Jung's view that some of the dream's fundamental symbols are actually an integral part of the human unconscious (archetypes) in the same way that fingers are a part of the hand.

Some inkling of the perceptual process involved in dreaming was noted as long ago as the writing of Aristotle:

> Impulses occurring in the daytime, if they are not very great and powerful, pass unnoticed because of greater waking impulses. But in the time of sleep the opposite takes place; for then small impulses seem to be great. This is clear from what often happens in sleep; men think that it is lightning and thundering when there are only faint echoes in their ears, and that they are enjoying honey and sweet flowers when only a drop of phlegm is slipping down their throats.

The dreamer has taken an element of reality and made it symbolic, given it a personal meaning, transformed it into part of his or her personal mythology. Few today would dream of honey and wildflowers as they did in Aristotle's time, and the personal meaning of the dream image will always be a function of individual psychic differences. But the dreaming *process* is the same, and this is where the scientific explanations begin to make sense.

The process is one of symbolizing what is perceived—investing it with meaning that is personal and creative. Reality is distorted, transformed in the process. What might have seemed unimportant in normal perception is suddenly very important in the dream image. What was only a small detail can suddenly become the most important part. Elements of separately perceived people or things can be combined. Animals can speak and objects can walk.

The understanding of this process actually came from several rather separate directions, all directed toward explaining the apparent similarity among dreams and other forms of unconscious activity. One understanding was provided by psychoanalysis, which had been urging acceptance of its solutions since the work of first Freud and then Jung in the 1920s. In Jung's view, as noted earlier, dreaming is one of the languages of the unconscious, hidden part of the self—a constant counterpart to the rational, verbal, logical side of consciousness. Jung postulated that through dreams, and through other forms of expression such as art, fairytales, myth, allegories, and so forth, unconscious processes reveal themselves on a routine basis. The physiological process of perception leading to this activ-- ity is identical with that of waking consciousness, and in both, images that come in through the eye are processed by brain centers that convert the image into a "meaningful" form; but the form is different in the inner part of the self, and the perceptual patterns of the brain centers that act on it are also quite distinct.

Besides psychoanalysis, another strong impetus for evolving a common model to explain all the different forms of illusion and hallucination is that they all share a strikingly common formula. Experiments actually have revealed four types of images found in large numbers of hallucinatory experiences: a grating, or lattice form; a cobweb-like form; a tunnel, funnel, or cone form; and a spiral form. Not only are the forms themselves similar (those who have migraine attacks or who have had hallucinogenic experiences will recognize them immediately), but they occur in a natural progression from the lattice shapes to the spiral as the hallucination progresses. Color changes occur in progression, too, shifting from blue at the beginning of the experience to reds, oranges, and yellows during the later stages.

In most hallucinatory experiences, this somewhat abstract form-perceiving period is followed by the visualization of "actual" images —derived from personal memory and therefore more meaningful. Again, there appears to be striking similarity among people reporting on these experiences. Some 70 percent claim to see religious symbols of some kind; nearly 50 percent see human figures or small animals (certainly true for Castaneda). Childhood memories and landscapes are also common, and can often be re-experienced and transformed into an active fantasy.

As in dreams, myths, and other forms of unconscious activity, "universal" symbols are far more commonplace in hallucinatory experiences than in ordinary consciousness—for example, visions of snakes, of sudden flashes of lightning, of the mandala symbol which in Eastern religions represents the wholeness of the universe and which Jung interpreted as the wholeness of self. The feelings and emotions accompanying these visions sometimes become so intense that words are inadequate to describe them. The true hallucination occurs, of course, when one believes that the visionary forms are real; but all the stages leading up to this total confusion between reality and imagination are equally intense.

A similar process can happen even with everyday memories. If you think back to a favorite time, chances are your remembrance contains an image of yourself doing something. Since you obviously couldn't see yourself in the original scene, the memory has been through a reworking not at all unlike that which produces a dream or hallucination.

Still another impetus for understanding the unconscious processes came from a purely scientific investigation—research into subliminal perception, which allows us to recognize stimuli below the thresholds of ordinary seeing, hearing, and so forth. Thresholds are present in every sensory system. In the case of touch, for example, thresholds are very easily demonstrated by the "two point" principle. If you simultaneously press two sharp points against the skin close together, they will be felt as a single point; as the points are moved farther and farther apart, however, a distance is reached at which the two are felt as separate sensations. This distance is the two-point threshold, and obviously relates to the sensitivity of the skin for this kind of stimulation.

Thresholds in hearing have to do with both the amount of energy in the auditory signal (its volume) and also the frequency of the vibrations. We generally cannot hear anything vibrating over 20,000 times per second (ultrasound), though dogs and many other species are sensitive in this region. Similarly, we cannot hear below 20 cycles per second.

Vision has similar thresholds. In the first place, a certain amount of light is required for an object to be seen (in order for the molecules on the surface of the object to receive enough energy to allow them to become stimulated and re-radiate energy back to the viewer). And the light must be of the frequency to which the human eye is sensitive.

Stimuli which fall below the perceptual threshold are therefore called subliminal, "below the limit." An object that is too dimly lit to be distinguished from the background is a subliminal visual stimulus, a sound too soft to be heard is subliminal to the auditory system, two points touched on the skin too close together to be felt separately are subliminal to touch, and so forth. It has been realized, however, as more and more comes to be known of the mechanisms of perception, that because subliminal stimuli are not consciously perceived by the ordinary sensory apparatus does not mean that they are not being perceived at all.

Instrumental in this new understanding was the observation that subliminal stimuli detected when awake have virtually the same effect on subsequent dreams as the supraliminal effects perceived when asleep have on concurrent dreams. In the same way that supraliminal perception is transformed into a personal dream symbol (the alarm clock bell into a church bell, for instance), so also do subliminal perceptions find their way into dreams.

The fact that subliminal images are perceived, although not consciously, can be demonstrated experimentally. Shown a subliminal image (a drawing flashed on the screen so quickly it is not even apparent that there has been any image at all), experimental subjects can be asked to describe what they have seen. When the researcher suggests that the subjects be free with their answers and take "wild guesses," subjects are often able to describe the object flashed on the screen even if they are unaware that they have seen anything— as if the image of the object simply materializes in their minds from nowhere. (Those told to be careful with their answers and to describe only what they are sure of do much less well, since their imaginations are deliberately inhibited.)

In addition to this kind of "guessing," however, another way to tell whether the subliminal stimulus has been received is to study dreams following exposure to subliminal images. The dream representation is often personalized, transformed into the dreamer's own personal vocabulary, distorted; but nevertheless it often represents the subliminal perception. (A dream about flying, for example, might follow exposure to a subliminal drawing of a kite.) The subliminal image, below the level of conscious perception, is unconsciously received, somehow triggering the subsequent dreaming process.

Especially important in these experiments is the observation that the dream image will occur only if the subject was not conscious of having seen the subliminal image at the time it was first presented. If a subject notices the image when it is presented, it will not occur in later dreams. But if the image is presented subliminally and not consciously perceived, the image will almost always show up later in the dream.

The ability to affect dreams through subliminal perceptions has led to speculation about the possibility of using subliminal messages to influence decisions by integrating them into various mass media productions. Vance Packard suggested in his book *The Hidden Persuaders* that Madison Avenue was engaged in a conscious effort to merchandise various products through the integration of hidden messages. Wilson Bryan Key, in *Subliminal Seduction,* made much the same point, supposedly demonstrating sexual and death symbols in the ice cubes of ads for alcoholic beverages, based on the idea that people drink primarily because of liberated sex drives or self-destructive urges and that these symbols would therefore stimulate increased drinking.

Key's premise supposes, of course, that the sex-symbol ice cubes were consciously created and are not merely the product of the author's own imagination. But even if the subliminal suggestion is intentional, can it have any effect? In one study, the word *beef* was flashed on the screen while an audience was watching an ordinary movie. Afterward they were asked to report whether they were hungry, and then to choose a sandwich. Many more said they were hungry as a result of the subliminal perception; but the percentage who chose a beef sandwich rather than another selection was not increased at all.

Thus it would seem that subliminal perception works at the level where the drive or the urge for something originates, rather than at the level where the drive has been translated into specific content. So in using subliminal suggestion in liquor ads Madison Avenue executives may be stimulating the self-destructive bent of the nation, or encouraging thirst, but they are probably not stimulating a desire for their clients' brand, and not even necessarily for alcohol.

The reason, according to a newly developed understanding of how unconscious stimulation and conscious awareness come about, is that two completely separate neurological pathways exist in the brain. One, made up of fast-conducting nerve fibers, is the well-understood "classical" sensory data pathway in which visual, auditory, and tactile information proceeds directly from the sense organ to the cerebral cortex and then to higher-order information-processing centers. Stimuli received along this pathway are those that immediately become conscious and are actually perceived. But data from a sense organ also proceed along another pathway, to the reticular ("network") activating system in the brain, an arrangement of constantly branching, highly interconnected nerve cells arranged like a column that runs through the middle of the brain.

The difference between the two pathways is illustrated when you are awakened by a single loud sound but can't remember what woke you. The sound has traveled extremely quickly into the brain from the ear to the primary cortex where it has been identified as a sound and responded to accordingly. But the message to the reticular center that causes wakefulness travels much, much more slowly, so that by the time you wake, the information about what woke you has already come and gone from the cortex. In other words, there is an actual neurological difference between the "information" contained in the stimulus (what the stimulus is) and awareness of the stimulus (its message to wake).

In experimental animals this difference is demonstrated by blocking the transmission of sensory data along the classical sensory pathways to the cortex. The experimenter can still arouse the animal from sleep by touching it or making a loud sound, even though no cortical brain activity is registered and the animal could not perceive anything. On the other hand, when the animal's reticular activating system is blocked, the animal cannot be roused from sleep even though its cortex is registering information as if it were actually perceiving it.

But as separate as these two systems are, it is their interrelationship that ultimately defines the state of waking consciousness. For the stimulus that affects the reticular portion of the brain can also, if it is strong enough, cause the transmission of nerve impulses that make the cortex (conscious) part of the brain lower its threshold for stimuli arriving from the sensory receptors. In the example of a continuous sound that wakes a sleeper, for instance, when the sound arrives at the cortex it is "asleep"—its threshold level has risen to the point where the sound does not cause alarm or a waking reaction. Simultaneously, the auditory data arrive at the reticular formation. If the sound is loud enough, the reticular formation transmits a message to the cortex telling it to lower its threshold. This, in turn, makes the cortex sensitive to the mainline flow of auditory information; one becomes conscious of the sound and awakes.

Thus, the subliminal perception can be defined as one in which the level of the stimulus is simply not strong enough to cause the reticular system to transmit a consciousness-arousing message to the cortex—or perhaps the message reaches the cortex too late.

What is perhaps most significant about this finding concerning the two brain centers is that it now appears to have a parallel in the difference between conscious and unconscious thought processes themselves. Just as the nerve impulses from the sense organs split into two separate pathways, so the brain processes information in two separate ways: consciously and unconsciously. Both kinds of thought occur simultaneously and both are in progress most of the time. The conscious processes—described as "secondary thought processes" because they involve higher-order processing—are more intense than the "primary thought processes" of unconscious activity. Conscious thought, acting on these more intense impulses, normally dominates the brain's functions. But as soon as conscious thought levels diminish, as happens in sleep, or the level of the stimulus drops below the threshold of conscious perception, as with subliminal perception, then the unconscious, symbolic, thought processes take over. It is exactly as Jung postulated: a separate but equal information-processing center that has an autonomous, *un*-conscious existence outside consciousness—the world of dreams and myths and imagination. In unconscious thought, as occurs during sleep, information is symbolic, connected with other events through a highly branched, associative kind of thinking; in the conscious thought of everyday life, the connections are direct. In unconscious thought, images are personalized; in consciousness, things are remembered "as they are."

This model helps explain what happens in sensory deprivation experiences, in which conscious stimulation is deliberately eliminated so that the subject's inner thought process comes to the fore —even though he/she is not actually sleeping. The experience of meditation, too, deliberately turns down the level of secondary thought processes so that the inner processes can be heard.

Also made clear is the effect of psychotropic drugs. Here the effect is chemical: the conscious thought processes are disorganized because of the pharmaceutical activity, and the unconscious thought process takes over. The images seen on a psychedelic "trip" are identical to the kinds of images seen while dreaming—except even more intensified.

Our model also helps explain why Don Juan was able to have such a profound effect on his disciple Castaneda. Through whatever means of magic Don Juan used—partially pharmacological, partly psychological—Castaneda's consciousness was turned off or turned down. This allowed Don Juan to communicate directly with Castaneda's unconscious mind.

Besides the differences in the types of images seen during periods of unconscious activity and ordinary, waking experience, there is also a profound difference in how the images are verbalized. Though we have already examined some of these differences in our discussion of language (Chapter 4), it is worth noting here that the dream/subliminal image appears to be associated with a less structured, less literal kind of meaning than is secondary, conscious cognition. One of the most striking examples occurs when experimental subjects are presented first with a subliminal image of a necktie, then a knee. In many cases, the images will be fused into a single concept associated through the sound of the words *tie* and *knee*—the word *tiny*.

Every word, of course, has many different associative fields or groups of concepts into which the word fits. *Tie* is related to a class of things worn around the neck, to another class of long, thin things, to another beginning with the letter *t*, to other verbs ("I *tie* the knot"), to other nouns ("I wear a *tie*"), to words rhyming with the "aye" sound, and so forth. In the primary thought process, the level at which unconscious thought activity occurs, no rules restrict how a word can be used. A dream in which a bus runs over something and breaks it ("The glass was *bus*-ted") is just as valid a use of the word *bus* as its "real" meaning. At the primary level, thoughts are linked by personal meanings—arranged in clusters that correspond to a person's own, self-developed thought processes. At this level, an incoming stimulus may trigger a whole succession of images that make absolutely no sense at the level of consciousness.

On the other hand, when *tie* or *bus* is used as part of a sentence, the word's meaning becomes defined by how it is used—its syntactic, grammatical meaning. In a sense, it is "locked into place" by other words that surround it, and rules such as agreement of subject with verb are in operation. While primary thought can associate *tie* with *tiny*, secondary thought takes its meaning much more literally.

Differences between primary and secondary thought also account for the difference between the meaning(s) of a word (defined by primary, unconscious thought) and the ability to name the object it represents (secondary, conscious thought). The dissociation happens naturally, in that one can guess the various associations which a subliminal image forms without necessarily being able to identify the image. Or it can happen in aphasia—a condition resulting from a brain injury in which the secondary thought process becomes inoperative. The patient is able to associate meanings together but cannot associate the meanings with any object nor verbalize the associations—a function normally performed by the conscious part of the brain.

Also related to the primary/secondary distinction is the observation that the Gestalt organization of incoming perceptions apparently happens *after* the data have found their way into the secondary thought process; the patterning doesn't operate at the unconscious level, where all types of combinations are possible and the "rules" for perceiving and organizing sensory data are not operative. This is also demonstrated by a set of experiments with reversible figures such as the duck/rabbit head shown on page 134. Secondary, conscious thought, where the Gestalt modeling takes place, can only perceive one or the other, rabbit or duck, since only one model can operate at once. But both interpretations occur simultaneously at the primary level since the laws of perceptual patterning do not operate there. Thus, if you were shown the reversible figure but didn't actually report seeing the duck's head, chances are you might have dreams involving a woodland scene or nature or even ducks, since the image has been perceived and is still "alive" in the unconscious memory until expressed in the dream. This is obviously similar to what happens when a subliminal image is not consciously noted but later appears in a dream, as described earlier.

We began our discussion of illusions with phenomena such as hallucinations which, though they do not correspond to an ordinary sense of reality because they are not part of conscious perception, are nonetheless "real." The hallucinations, dreams, reversible figure phenomena, and other manifestations of unconscious/primary thought are not the only examples of perception that seem to offer an expanded, enhanced sense of reality, however. One of the most common forms of "expanded" perception is eidetic imagery (from the Greek word *eidos,* or image). Those gifted with eidetic ability can actually hold an image in their minds for at least two to five minutes after the source of the image has been removed. In the United States, some 5 percent of children ages six to twelve have this ability, decreasing to virtually no adults. In non-Western countries, however, many more people seem to have this ability, both adults and children.

Eidetic perception is not the result of an afterimage somehow "burned into the retina," nor the result of "photographic memory." Rather, it is the unique ability to actually perceive the picture as if it were in front of you, so real you can scan it with your eyes. Then, after a few minutes, it disappears again.

Lest there be any doubt that the image is actually seen by an eidetic child and not just described from ordinary memory, a simple test can be performed. Show the child a line drawing of a steamship with birds and clouds. Remove the image after several seconds, wait a few minutes, and then show the child a second drawing of wavy lines and a mustache. In many cases the eidetic person will be able to fuse the two drawings together, suddenly seeing the image of a face—a kind of joining similar to that in the tie and knee rebus discussed earlier. Here the fusion is based on purely visual eidetic memory, which still holds the first image of the steamship while the second is being presented.

Not all children who are eidetic can perform this mental fusing, however, so there are other tests to show the difference between eidetic ability and ordinary memory. We can all describe pictures we know well from memory, and so can the eidetic child. But if the eidetic person is shown a familiar image for only a few seconds—shorter than the ten-second period needed to form an eidetic image in the brain—then the child will report that he/she can see nothing. In using the ordinary process of memory, of course, the eidetic child, having seen the image only briefly, can call up the mental image of the familiar picture which can then be described. But the eidetic process is short-circuited. It is also true that if an eidetic child looks at an image with only one eye, then no eidetic image can be seen by the other eye, whereas there is no such restriction with ordinary visual memory.

Again, when both normal and eidetic children describe a picture from ordinary memory, the description becomes less and less confident as the child must search more and more deeply into the memory to continue with the description. But the eidetic child's description of an eidetic image sounds completely confident all the way through—exactly as if the picture were in front of him. But when the picture fades from eidetic memory, the image is gone and cannot be brought back.

The eidetic process can be thwarted if various kinds of mental "tricks" are used. Conscious, rapid eye blinking will cause an eidetic image to disappear. And if the child consciously thinks about the image during the first viewing, or verbally describes it, then no eidetic image is formed in the first place.

The whole subject of eidetic imagery has for some time been relegated to the realm of "mysticism" and "unreality"—partly due to the nasty political overtones created when scientists of the German Third Reich tried to claim eidetic ability as a characteristic of the "master race." Nonetheless, it is once again receiving scientific attention.

Perhaps the most cogent explanation of the eidetic process is that it is a unique form of visual memory. The eidetic image is remembered exactly as it was seen—without the embellishments of personal association that characterize ordinary memories. It is as if a person with eidetic ability is able to read an image in immediate short-term visual memory. Thus, the eidetic image definitely occurs in a fairly rigid time frame. It lasts only for a specific period before it begins fading, and the part of the image seen first begins fading faster than parts of the image seen later.

Still another sensory phenomenon only just being discovered is synesthesia—the crossing over from one sensory system to another so that sounds are seen, smells heard, feelings perceived visually, and so forth.

Synesthesia is related to some relatively widespread, "normal" sensory experiences. Many, for example, associate the color blue with coolness and the color red with excitement and heat. High-pitched, squeaky sounds are often associated with small objects while deeper, fuller sounds are associated with larger, fuller objects. Similarly, poets working with "tone poems" use the sounds of words to evoke visual and sensory experiences at the same time that the words keep their dictionary meanings. It could be said that all poetry reflects a synesthetic experience in which the sounds of the words cross over from the auditory to the visual system and evoke visual images.

True synesthesia, however, has a much more powerful effect—as if the person with auditory/visual synesthesia carries a "light organ" around in his head that constantly responds to the sounds of the environment and produces vivid, very "real" colors, not in the imagination, but in the actual visual field. For the nonsynesthete, of course, the crossovers are just an illusion; but for the synesthete, they are actually seen by the eyes.

There are as many different crossover possibilities as there are sensory systems—links between taste and hearing, touch and smell, hearing and smelling, and so forth. But the most common crossover is the link between hearing and vision through which sounds are seen. Not only is this experience not uncommon, but among synesthetes there is quite a bit of agreement on the specific colors and images evoked by different sounds. By far the most common perception is that human speech evokes the most vivid visual response, and that within speech, vowel sounds are the most clearly perceived. Even within the vowel sounds themselves there is considerable agreement among synesthetes: red, for example, is evoked most often by the [α] sound in *bottle* and the [o:] sound in *boat*. Yellow is associated with the [e] in *bate* and to a lesser extent the [i] in *beet*. The [u] in *boot* is most often seen as a brown color. White, on the other hand, is most often associated with the sounds [a] and [i:]. In general, the pattern appears to be that the higher, tighter, more compressed vowel sounds stimulate white, yellow, and the brighter colors, whereas brown, black, and more somber colors are most often seen as the result of longer vowel sound stimulation.

Synesthesia is a sensory experience with a name and a growing body of "scientific evidence" supporting the view that it is not simply the over-excited imagination of people who claim to be sensitive or gifted. Synesthesia is thus linked to all the other sensory phenomena that were once thought to be the devil's work, part of the unconscious, and therefore not a part of natural, "good" human activity. Modern science reveals, however, that quite the reverse may be true: given the limitations of human sensory systems and the existence of so many processes that are not part of "normal," conscious thought, "normal reality" itself may be a questionable observation.

And, waiting in the wings to be explained by science, is a group

of experiences known as extra-sensory perception for which absolutely no body of scientific knowledge or even a rational explanation
exists yet. Extra-sensory perception is as weird to us today as dreams
and hallucinations were once to our Medieval predecessors. But can
we therefore discount ESP simply because there is no scientific
explanation of it yet?

Chapter Nine
Extra-Sensory Perception

> For the cherub with his flaming sword is hereby commanded to leave his guard at the tree of life, and when he does the whole creation will be consumed, and appear infinite and holy whereas now it appears finite and corrupt.
>
> This will come about by an improvement of sensual enjoyment. . . .
>
> If the doors of perception were cleansed every thing would appear to man as it is, infinite.
>
> For man has closed himself up till he sees all things through narrow chinks of his cavern.
>
> William Blake, THE MARRIAGE OF HEAVEN AND HELL

Adam and Eve in the Garden of Eden were in perfect harmony with the entirety of nature. They sang with the birds, ran with the deer. So perfect was this union that they knew the inner essence of all things, could communicate with creatures in their own languages, could name them with their proper names. Then something terrible happened: the serpent came between man and nature. Symbol of the very human desire to know more, to see from the outside, to establish oneself in relation to other things, it brought paradise to an end and the human species was born.

We offer this interpretation of the myth of Adam and Eve not because of what it might say about the past, but rather as an archetype of a very present reality—the seemingly cross-cultural, perhaps universal desire to return to the garden where things were once perfectly protected, perfectly harmonious, perfectly at peace. And, once back in the garden, communication between man and nature could presumably be reinstated. We could know, without knowing how we knew, every secret of the universe.

The situation recounted in the early Babylonian story *The Epic of Gilgamesh* is almost identical:

> So the goddess conceived an image in her mind and it was of the stuff of Anu of the firmament. She dipped her hands in water and pinched off clay, she let it fall in the wilderness, and noble Enkidu was created. . . . His body was rough, he had long hair like a woman's. It waved like the hair of the goddess of corn. His body was covered with hair, like the god of cattle. He was innocent of mankind; he knew nothing of the cultivated land.
>
> Enkidu ate grass in the hills with the gazelle and lurked with wild beasts at water holes; he had joy of the water with the herds of wild game. . . .
>
> So the trapper set out on his journey to Uruk and addressed himself to Gilgamesh saying, "A man [Enkidu] unlike any other is roaming now in the pastures; he is as strong as a star from heaven and I am afraid to approach him. He helps the wild game to escape; he fills in my pits and pulls up my traps." Gilgamesh said, "Trapper, go back, take with you a harlot, a child of pleasure. At the drinking-hole she will strip, and when he sees her beckoning he will embrace her and the game of the wilderness will surely reject him."

The loss of innocence. The breakdown of communication between mother and child, between the individual and the cosmos. Man achieves his own identity and in the process loses touch with the nature/mother that spawned him, making it impossible to return to the garden and the womb.

But wait. All is not lost. Some say there is a way we can again be in harmony with nature. Talk with dead spirits. Know what is going to be said before it is made conscious and vocalized. Intuit with precise accuracy if any mean us harm. And feel the future as if it were the present because of the timeless sense in which time is not linear at all but more spiraform or circular instead. It is even possible to break down the barrier between life and death so that reincarnation becomes a possibility. These are the experiences, of course, which fall within the realm of parapsychology, extra-sensory perception, and psychic phenomena.

These "mysterious events" can be interpreted quite simply as a harkening back to a time when things were more perfect, when communication happened naturally, when *everything* about nature could be known by the human senses, which have subsequently become clouded over by death and knowledge (the two trees of Eden). The psychic, in a state like the one before the fall, sees all, knows all, feels things on a different, perhaps more expanded level than normal. The future and the past become one.

This was the case with William Thomas Wolfe, a psychic but ordinary man living with his wife and two sons in upstate New York, who discovered one day that he could perceive things on a very extraordinary level.

I started meditating more and more, and as I did I noticed I could often understand what someone was going to say shortly before they said it. It was like living in a reverberation chamber or perhaps in a can of oil. . . . I don't know exactly how to describe it, but I discovered I could do more than just listen to someone talk and evaluate what they were saying. It was like an in-depth experience of what was going on at the time.

Other strange things began happening as well . . . heat at various spots in my head, very pleasurable sensations, and so forth. I also began to get involved in other kinds of activities such as biofeedback as an extension of my meditation. And I began reading books trying to figure out exactly what was happening to me and looking for a model to try to explain some of these things. The model I found was Kundalini yoga.

This all led up to an experience one night when I had just gone to bed and was lying there perfectly awake. All of a sudden I just exploded into another state of being. It was like some sort of an electrical effect in that I was no longer experiencing things or sensing things from the standpoint of an ordinary physical person. I had become a completely different being, no longer a two-legged, two-armed human, but part of a complex of silvery balls just hanging in space. I experienced only blackness, only the existence of the silver balls, which were part of me, extending out into somewhere. You might say it was like the view of someone sitting on an atom. Somehow my consciousness got totally wrapped up in something completely different.

One of the things that happened for some time afterwards is what I call "feelies." This was also some sort of an electrical effect where I would experience something internally that would then actually happen later. What I experienced was not just a reflection of what was going to take place, however. I was actually experiencing the event, but in a slightly different way than I would later on. It's as though there were two valid points of reality for a given incident.

In experiencing something on the front end and then experiencing it again at the second point, it becomes very difficult to distinguish which is the true reality, which came first. You begin to have questions about what time is all about, and how does it relate to events. After going through something like this it throws you into a different mind set. . . .

Related to this is the question of whether we perceive what happens or whether we make it happen to correspond to what we perceive. I believe that perception is a little bit of both, that perception itself can actually go outward rather than just flowing in as most people believe. I think that perceptions themselves can be constructive acts in the ongoing creation of everything around us—that's one way I have to explain some of the things that happened to me.

What can science add to this interpretation? For psychic investigators, the answer is, not much. For science has a long history of being the debunker when it comes to psychic phenomena, pointing out time and time again that the various aspects of telepathy, precognition, psychokinesis, and so on cannot possibly be so. For the genuine psychic or even the person who has an occasional precognitive experience, on the other hand, the phenomena are very real— as real as "normal" perceptions themselves. And so science and the psychic have been at odds over the centuries.

Psychics, of course, have not been exactly cooperative in helping scientists investigate parapsychological phenomena. "These things aren't rational and scientific," they stress, rejecting even the very desire on the part of science to "validate" their findings. Then there are the crude fortune tellers and show-business "guess what's in my hand" acts which, while fostering an image that psychic powers are involved, are merely magical deception. The most recent case was that of two young magicians who embarrassed the whole psychic community by presenting themselves as having paranormal abilities, then revealing the magician's tricks they used after scientists had certified them as genuine psychics.

Nevertheless, in spite of all the hoaxes, there is indeed a body of very real data that has been accumulated about psychic experiences. A story is told about Winston Churchill who, during World War II, made frequent trips out to the line to boost the morale of his troops. Each day his driver would pick him up, open the car door for him, and Churchill would get in. But one day, Churchill refused the open door and went around to the other side of the car. As he was being sped along to his destination, a bomb went off immediately alongside the car, throwing it onto two wheels; miraculously, it righted itself without overturning. Churchill's weight caused the car to right itself—weight that would have been on the wrong side of the car if he had followed his normal routine. Later he revealed that he had heard a voice saying, "Stop. Go around to the other side and get in there," when it had been time to get into the car.

Another experience is described in the *Journal of Parapsychology:*

A mother had a waking picture of her elder son, Herbert, dead in the bathtub. It haunted her so much that she made a special point of listening that nothing went wrong. But she did not tell him her impression, though she told her younger son Peter.

After a couple of years, Herbert went away. And when he came home for a holiday she still remembered it [her vision]. One evening on this visit she heard him whistling and singing in the bathtub. She was dressed to go out but could not leave. After a while she heard the water running out but did not hear him singing, so she opened the door. And there he lay, exactly as she had seen him two years before. There was gas heat and the window was closed and he had apparently been overcome by fumes. She immediately opened the door and windows and called the doctor, and Herbert was revived. If she had not been there he doubtless would have died.

Still another experience, recounted in R. Crookwall's *More Astral Projections,* seems to record another fairly common psi (psychic) phenomenon—the out-of-body experience in which a person senses that his or her "soul" or consciousness has somehow become separated from the reality of the physical body. This is similar to the experience recounted by those who have had close encounters with death or who have actually survived a death experience.

On Sunday, the ninth of November, a few minutes after midnight, I began to feel very ill, and by two o'clock was definitely suffering from acute gastroenteritis, which kept me vomiting and purging until about eight o'clock in the morning. By ten o'clock, I had developed all the symptoms of acute poisoning. . . . I wanted to ring for assistance, but found I could not, and so quite placidly gave up the attempt. I realized I was very ill and very quickly reviewed my financial position. Thereafter at no time did my consciousness appear to be in any way dimmed, but I suddenly realized that *my* consciousness was separating from another consciousness that was also me. These, for purposes of description, I could call the A and the B consciousnesses, and throughout what follows, the ego attached itself to the A consciousness.

The B personality I recognized as belonging to the body, and as my physical condition grew worse and the heart was fibrillating rather than beating, I realized that the B consciousness belonging to the body was beginning to show signs of being composite—that is, built up of "consciousnesses" from the head, the heart and the viscera. These components became more individual and the B consciousness began to disintegrate, while the A consciousness, which was now me, seemed to be altogether outside my body, which it could see.

Gradually I realized I could see not only my body and the bed in which it was, but everything in the whole house and garden, and then realized that I was seeing not only "things" at home, but in London and Scotland, in fact wherever my attention was directed, it seemed to me; and the explanation which I received, from what source I do not know, but which I found myself calling to myself my *mentor,* was that I was free in a time dimension of space, wherein "now" was in some way equivalent to "here" in the ordinary three-dimensional space of everyday life.

Almost everyone, it might be pointed out, has had the experience of "feeling" they are being stared at, then turning around and discovering that this is indeed true. Or of concentrating on getting someone's attention by projecting energy toward them and "willing" them to turn around—often successfully. The Rosicrucians, of course, claim that thoughts have wings, and indeed they do seem to in these cases.

Many of these things do continue to baffle modern science, and the tendency is still to reject what cannot be explained with the current set of scientific laws. Remembering, however, that acupuncture was once vilified by the medical community but is now standard practice in many hospitals, and that the theories of men such as Alfred Wegener (who developed the idea of continental drift) and Charles Darwin were once ridiculed and rejected, science today is a little more open. For some psi phenomena, science has developed some degree of acceptance and, in some cases, has at least partial explanations of how they work. And for others, such as reincarnation, it is developing a "We don't understand it now but let's wait and see" attitude.

One of the first realizations provided by science is that just as there is a great multiplicity of sensory experiences so there is a multiplicity of extra-sensory perceptions as well. They fall into certain categories and, like any other phenomena, each category has its own set of experiences. Broadly speaking, these categories are: auras and experiencing "other parts" of people than the normal, corporal body; precognitive and telepathic experiences, in which a person experiences something without immediate physical reference; psychokinesis, in which objects are moved by mental powers; and experiencing apparitions and spirits, usually manifestations of dead people.

Based on conversations with those who have had psi experiences, our suggestion is, quite simply, that ESP is exactly what its name suggests: *extra*-sensory perception, truly a "sixth sense" about things or, perhaps, a sixteenth or seventeenth sense. Not the result of hidden forces from an unknown source. Not the mystical claptrap that has been associated with ESP and psychic ability throughout the ages. Not a weird blend of magic and witchcraft. But a very human experience in which sensory signals are transmitted and received by the body that are either below the normal threshold of a known sensory system or else are a form of energy that is being detected by a sense that we are unaware of at present. In other words, just because the various forms of ESP lie outside our current ability to describe them does not mean that they will not, one day, be as rational and "scientific" as acupuncture is today.

It is less likely, of course, that there will ever be a rational explanation for what lies on the other side of death, though this is a big part of psychic phenomena. Reincarnation and ghostly apparitions are, naturally, the hardest phenomena for a scientist to accept. But the various other manifestations of psychic ability fall well within the boundaries of what can be incorporated by modern science. And indeed, several of the phenomena that are considered "mysterious" could possibly be explained using known scientific principles.

A fairly clear example is the ability of some to "dowse" for water. A person holds a "divining rod" (a forked stick) out in front of the body, then walks until the rod supposedly dips down of its own accord, indicating that water lies just below the ground. Pure fallacy? Perhaps in some cases the diviners were tipped off by land surveys. But certainly not in enough cases to explain the uncanny accuracy many diviners experience.

First one must, with an open mind, acknowledge the phenomenon. Then it becomes possible to examine what might have caused it. The explanation many are coming to accept is that these people may share birds' sensitivity to magnetic fluctuations in the earth's surface. Increased sensitivity to this kind of energy would almost surely make them sensitive to the magnetic fluctuation that a large body of underground water would create. And their arm muscles, tired of holding the stick out in front of them, might then twitch when they felt the difference.

The existence of this particular magnetic sensitivity has yet to be demonstrated conclusively in man. In his book *Human Navigation and the Sixth Sense,* however, Robin Baker reveals his experiments in which groups of blindfolded people were set free at some distance from their homes, then asked to begin walking toward where they assumed home to be. Although Baker's experiments have yet to be replicated by other scientists, his findings are that humans *can* use magnetic fields as an aid to navigation in the absence of visual cues. The existence of this sense in other animal species has definitely been demonstrated, and it may be only a matter of time before it is proven in man. For it is unlikely that the gravitational flux of the earth is a force to which we are not sensitive in any way.

It is interesting to note in this regard that many cultures, including the Chinese, believe quite strongly that the orientation of buildings and homes to the earth's north/south axis is vital for health and well-being.

The existence of magnetic sensitivity is reinforced by another astonishing and *proven* finding about people which may help explain the perception of auras, halos or projected images that some can perceive around the heads of others. The brain's electrical activity has, of course, been measurable for many years now thanks to the EEG (electroencephalograph), a device that measures the overall electrical activity of the brain. But by using a newly-developed device known as a SQUID (superconducting quantum interference device), researchers such as Lloyd Kaufman and his colleagues at New York University can now actually measure extremely fine electrical activity in the brain from just above the scalp. Moreover, the shifts in brain activity that result from different types of thought can also be recorded and mapped with this instrument. The ability to detect how the brain processes information, which part is involved in pattern recognition, which part in problem solving, and so forth, is obviously exciting. But it also suggests the truly startling idea that the activity of the brain may actually project out beyond the scalp. In other words, in addition to whatever our bodies and faces do to reflect our thoughts, the brain itself may be signaling what it is thinking to the outside world. And it may be possible to actually detect and measure these signals as a kind of aura surrounding the head.

Is this, then, the aura that psychics detect, an image of a person's inner mental state reflected in an electromagnetic energy field projected from his head? Someone with the ability to consciously or unconsciously "read" a person's mental state from this radiation would therefore be neither weird nor endowed with mystical ability to communicate with the spirit world, but simply endowed with extra-sensory powers. And, as one can train oneself to detect finer gradations in sounds or tastes, so the psychic trains himself or herself to be more aware of these readings.

This is the case with Lynn Walcutt, a psychic and healer who lives in New York City, describing her very "special" abilities:

> To sense what someone might need, I first "tune in," aligning and merging myself with their energy—as if I become them. It's a physical sensation, feeling within myself their physical sensations.
>
> Symbols will come to my mind. Some of them are concrete—I'll see someone in an airplane, for example. That doesn't necessarily signify that they will actually be in an airplane (though often it does), but that they are taking a journey of some type—whether it's in consciousness, or they're on a spiritual path.
>
> Other times I will get geometric forms around people—for instance, a pyramid around someone who has had an incarnation in Egypt or whose consciousness goes in the direction of some type of mystical pursuit. If I see a big eye image over someone, that person is usually studying with a spiritual master.
>
> Sometimes these symbols and auras are external—they look like radiating energy you can actually touch. But they can also be internal, like dream images which can be visualized by closing your eyes.
>
> The difference between being psychic and being intuitive is that the psychic actually senses energy—sees things, hears things, smells things, and so forth, whereas intuition is more about feeling things. Almost anyone can have intuitive feelings—just "knowing" that something is wrong or that something has happened. But being

psychic requires a special ability; when I have psychic perceptions, I think I am sensing something completely different from ordinary perception.

This is especially true for colors. For instance, red for me is a very active color. Fire engine red shows vitality, physical energy—it's related to the first chakra [energy center in Buddhism and other eastern religions]. Burning red or scarlet around someone's body shows irritation . . . inflammation . . . someone who's angry. When I see someone angry, the red shoots blotches or sparks around them—it's not just a field. Living in a red environment will stimulate the base, physical self.

A bright, vibrant green is a healing color, and is also the color of the heart. If there's a murky green around someone, it will show some imbalance in the physical body. Green is related to physical emotions.

Orange around someone is a very special color. A lot of actors and actresses have orange around them, and people involved in public relations. It's an outgoing energy—a second- and some third-chakra energy. Orange also shows a lot of nervous energy and can be over-stimulating.

When I get yellow around someone I see it as an intellectual color, which is also related to the third chakra. It's reasoning ability or writing ability. Yellow will show around someone who's very sensitive and also has that reasoning ability.

Sky blue is the color of the throat chakra, which represents creativity, musical ability, ability to communicate . . . creative energy. That shade of blue I'll see around teachers, counselors, psychologists, people who talk and use their voice for some type of healing.

Indigo is a deep blue that shows intuition—psychic ability, intuitive ability, ability to just know things and not know where they come from. It's the shade of blue you'll see around spiritual masters and teachers—people who are teaching on a spiritual level.

The crown chakra at the top of the head is violet, representing total cosmic awareness, or just total bliss. Violet shows that a person is on a path of service, but it will also show around creative artists and schizophrenics. Violet is a healing color to the nervous system.

These colors aren't just my personal vision. I think that anyone who is really clairvoyant will see them also because they have universal meanings. My experience working with people's auras is that they always fit. I'll see yellow and it turns out that the person is almost always a rational type, often with writing ability.

The colors can also be used. Color is just light radiating at that particular vibration level. And when you look at it, it goes through your eyes and affects a part of the nervous system responsive to that particular vibration—it brings out a chemical reaction in the endocrine glands.

It's like there's a web, a field of energy. And colors affect the subtle energy field which then has a stimulating effect on the body's physical energy field.

Seeing something green affects the thymus—it's a rejuvenating or balancing force that acts in the middle of the body. Yellow would affect the solar plexus and the adrenal glands in the kidneys. Black is a neutralizer somehow—after a while you'd probably get really drained if you saw black all the time. Blue affects the thyroid. Violet affects the pituitary gland. Deeper blue affects the pineal gland. Red affects the plexus of nerves at the base of the spine—an activating color.

I use color in my healing. I'll imagine that there are beams of light coming through my hands and fingers and flowing into a person. For instance, if someone is very upset, I'll use the color blue or turquoise. Now turquiose is good for the nervous system—a combination of blue, which constricts the blood vessels, and green, which is very good for the nervous system and for the skin. Or if someone has a headache, I'll put my hands on their head and imagine that I'm beaming in a blue light. And I'll also have them visualize blue around them. If someone's depressed, I use red and orange.

Sometimes, if I want to transmute someone's energy, I'll breathe in the red that I see around them—or whatever color is a disturbing element. I'll breathe it into myself, down into my stomach, see it changing color, and breathe it back out at them. Usually within fifteen minutes the mood changes.

I worked up in Vermont for two years with a girl who was born with no eyes. She learned to perceive color through its feel. At first I would give her different things that were red and then I would describe red heat-wise. Red is a visually hot color, but when you feel it or perceive it, it is a slower vibration; blue is visually cooler and creates a cool sensation. Then the blind girl and I worked with red and blue paper, identical except for their inks. She learned how

to identify them by touch and then to walk up to someone in class
and know what colors they were wearing.

Response to an area of the electromagnetic spectrum which is
outside the range of normal sensitivity may account for another psi-
type but more universally accepted phenomenon—the effect of colors on mood. We noted in Chapter 5 that the relationship between
a color such as red and a meaning such as "stop" is purely symbolic
and arbitrary. But there may be something more to the relationship,
a different level in which the color has a direct effect on some
fundamental physiological and emotional reactions. Many religions
and cults are quite specific in attributing certain colors to certain
emotional states. Yoga, for instance, divides the body into chakras
(energy centers), and assigns a color to each. The same kind of
system was plotted in the Cabala, the ancient mystical text based
on an interpretation of Hebrew scriptures, for the spheres on the
"tree of life" which represents the human experience. A set of colors
is also prescribed for the various cards in the Tarot deck. And the
alchemists postulated a set of colors that corresponded with the
chemical elements and could be mixed together to form new colors
just like the chemicals themselves.

As Jung has shown throughout his work, the various symbols of
the alchemical process are all connected with deep-rooted psychological processes. And in all these color systems, the colors themselves are given emotional values corresponding to other elements
in the system. Yoga, for instance, assigns the color blue to the
chakra in the head. Blue is therefore said to be an intellectual color,
a color associated with writing and literary pursuits, and general
intellectual thought. And it predicts both that writers will associate
themselves with the color blue and that thinking about the color or
having it nearby will stimulate intellectual thought.

The tendency, of course, is to dismiss these color correspondences
in the same way one would debunk the assignment of special gem-
stones to certain months. But there is a possibility, at this point
somewhat conjectural and not yet tested, that colors may actually
be more than passive elements in the environment—nice to look at

but of little other significance. The discipline known as photobiology is attempting to establish that the connection between the human organism and the colors is just as important as the connection of humans with light itself.

Others besides scientists, of course, have long recognized the emotional value of colors. Cinematographer Vittorio Storaro, for example, who won an Academy Award for *Apocalypse Now,* uses the colors of lights to add mood to the scenes he shoots:

I am a photographer, which originally meant "writing with light." That is the basis of my work—trying to write the story of the film with a beam of light which is the combination of all the colors. I work with colors and light to try and make the story of the film take place on a very unconscious level, the level at which color and light affect the body directly. So you can experience the film's emotions through the symbolism of the colors and the ideas of the photography. . . .

In *Last Tango in Paris,* I was trying to deal with specific color vibrations as part of the story. There was a kind of conflict between male and female, daylight and nightlight, artificial energy and natural energy. These were the two different worlds that the characters were living in.

Apocalypse Now was the sum of my past and present work—everything that I had done in the past, everything that I could do in the present. But it drained me, and after I was finished I had to take it easy for a while, I had to recharge my battery. During this time I started to do research once again, studying like a student and looking through all my books, into the meaning of colors.

This was work that led up to *Luna,* which was clearly a movie with an idea of analysis inside it. That's why I went to the symbolism of the colors, their meanings. In psychoanalysis, every color means something different—red is a passionate color, blue is a color of intellectualism, and so forth. If you dream about something in color, it has a specific meaning. So I was trying to understand these meanings and use them in the film.

I also came to realize through my studies that some of the choices I had made earlier about colors were an unconscious reflection of this symbolism. There was a reason why I had chosen to do *The*

Conformist in blue. And why I had selected orange as the color to represent artificial energy in *The Last Tango*—going with the warm tones of the wintertime sun, the color of the apartment, and so on. I came to realize what color means.

It's very clear that all the warm color, the oranges, in *Last Tango* were about the masculine, about the sun, about the kind of energy that is very powerful. It means passion. It means activity. It means something very strong.

Blue in *The Conformist* is the color of freedom, because blue is the color of the spirit of the intellectual. It is also the color of the moon, the mother, the female in *Luna*. It is about the soul—a more introspective color.

After these realizations, my work with color and light became a lot more conscious. This is why in *One From the Heart* I wanted to work with the *physiology* of color—its direct effect on the body. It was a movie about emotions, about feelings between people. So I wanted to show the reaction of the body itself in the presence of one color or another.

This is true—scientists have proved it. If you expose the body to light, then it becomes more active. If you expose it to darkness, it becomes less active. That is why we wake and sleep. And the first impression I had of Las Vegas was that no one ever sleeps there— which is why they keep all the lights on all the time, to keep people stimulated and awake.

Television commercials are also like that—they use light and dark and colors to influence the mind. Some of the information in commercials, of course, is very valuable. But the other side is that they are constantly bombarding the mind with images and colors that have a direct effect on the viewer. I do not think that is so healthy.

There is no doubt that we are living in the century of the image. My children are playing with video games. Images are the simplest way to communicate with people—from the time that the first man scratched on the wall of a cave. We are surrounded by image. And color is a simple language that everybody can understand. For children, the most simple language is cartoons, which are lines that symbolize a man, a woman, etc. And through the color you give to them you put on top of them a symbol. Something that you can understand very fast. Because your body reacts in the presence of green or red in completely different ways.

We have already established, of course, that color is electromagnetic radiation of a certain narrow range of frequencies, and that it is registered by the retina when the pigments in cone cells absorb energy stimulated by wavelengths representing the primary colors red, green and blue. So it is already proven that color influences a chemical reaction in the body, and that the reaction for one color is different from that for another.

It is also fairly clear that we are sensitive to electromagnetic radiation even outside the range of visible light in much the same way. With microwaves, for example, and even with the type of radio frequency (RF) radiation that is used to transmit radio and television signals, the body absorbs the radiation and its cells react. On the most basic level, of course, the body simply absorbs the energy as pure heat, and the cells of the human body can cook in a radiation-filled environment just as food heats in a microwave oven. This is why such precautions are taken to place glass in front of the television screen, and why a television should never be operated without one.

Many scientists, especially those in the USSR, also believe that the body absorbs this kind of RF radiation into its various organs where they claim it has truly destructive effects—chromosome damage in the testes, actual retinal damage, changes perhaps to the composition of the white cells in the bloodstream, and other disturbances in the body's immune system.

The current question of the photobiologists and those who are attempting to use color to achieve various psychological effects—color therapists—is whether there are additional biochemical reactions happening simultaneously with actual color vision in the cones, reactions that have enormously powerful effects on emotions. They could be taking place at the retinal level. Or, as the nerve impulses signaling "red," "green," and "blue" travel back to the visual cortex in the brain, perhaps they make contact with other nerves that carry the information to a brain center which stimulates emotional response.

But the eye itself need not be involved. Color, like microwave and RF radiation detection, may also be sensed by a completely separate process, such as directly through the skin. One researcher went into a schoolroom for handicapped children and did some new interior decorating. An orange carpet was changed to gray, and the wall colors were changed to royal blue and light blue from their original orange and white colors. The seven children in the class responded unconsciously, their blood pressure dropping an average of 17 percent. Most startling of all, two of the children who achieved the drop were blind. It is possible, of course, that they simply responded to the changed behavior of their sighted class-mates. But the other explanation—that nonvisual processes were involved—is quite intriguing. The possible mechanisms are numer-ous. The color could cause the release of a hormone or prevent a hormone from being produced. It could supply energy for a chemi-cal reaction that allows an influential enzyme to be produced. But for the present, this is still in the realm of speculation.

There is one key area, however, in which science has actually proved some of the thinking of those with a mystical bent, namely in research on the human pineal gland. Because it is in a relatively primitive part of the brain, because it is the only structure in the brain which is not bilaterally symmetrical, because it appears to be a lonely, individual organ surrounded by the greater mass of the other brain structures, the pineal gland has attracted the attention of mystics and philosophers.

Descartes claimed it as the seat of the human soul, thinking it was here that the corporal activity of muscle movement came to-gether with the thinking activity of the brain. This led to the hypothesis that it was in the pineal that spinal fluid was made—the supposed medium of exchange between body and soul. In Eastern religions, the pineal is considered a true "third eye," the means by which the inner self sees the light of the world and divine revelation. An exercise in yoga is to close your eyes and have someone hold his index finger about a half inch away from the middle of your fore-head; many see a bright area of light, indicating that the pineal has been stimulated (or that one has received divine inspiration and knowledge).

More modern mystics exercise great creativity in describing the functions of the pineal gland, claiming it as the "inner eye" whose function is to see the mystical light within the soul. And some even believe that shining a small flashlight at the middle of the forehead will stimulate the pineal to function better.

Science has, very recently, come to a fairly clear understanding of how the pineal works in animals such as lizards and birds. It serves primarily as a synchronizing clock, keeping the animal's internal body rhythms aligned with the natural changes in day length as the year progresses (see Chapter 3). It is also evident that in lizards the pineal works as an actual "eye," sensitive not to visual images but to illumination and apparently to the angle of the sun's rays (their polarization) as the light falls on the earth.

The real surprise has been, however, that this tiny pea-shaped organ located in one of the most primitive parts of our brain has just as profound an effect on humans as it does on animals. The action in humans is virtually the same as that in animals outlined in Chapter 3: the pineal hormone melatonin, inhibited when it is light and secreted when it is dark, regulates the body's activity levels and is probably the mechanism that causes sleep and drowsiness when nighttime stimulates its production.

Even more important, melatonin governs the activity of the sex organs and therefore sexual activity itself. Like so many other species, the human animal's urge to mate may be affected by seasonal cues. We assume that the flirtatious mood many feel in the springtime is a result of the warm air and the cheeriness of the birds. More likely, it now seems, it is because the longer day length changes the melatonin balance and the sex organs begin growing more active. The melatonin produced by the pineal may also help to explain why children in tropical climates seem to reach puberty more quickly than children in northern climates, since they are exposed to a good deal more sunlight and therefore produce less melatonin to inhibit the gonads.

The same kinds of effects can be noticed on a daily basis. Again the fluctuations in the size of the gonads and sexual activity are linked with melatonin production and thence to the pineal. As is the case with the yearly cycles, daylight prevents the production of melatonin and therefore allows the sex organs to reach their greatest activity during the daytime. Favorite times for enjoying sex differ widely; but current biochemical thinking about the pineal shows that nature probably makes it better in the morning and during the day rather than at night.

The only difference between humans and lizards in this respect is that while the lizard can sense the presence of light or darkness directly with its third eye, humans appear to rely solely on input from their normal eyes to sense the presence or absence of light. Stimulation of the eye with light causes release of noradrenaline in the sympathetic nervous system. This substance, in turn, blocks the production of the enzyme used by the pineal to synthesize the melatonin. Without melatonin in the bloodstream, the gonads are free to function at full scale, producing more sex hormones. And the sex hormones, in turn, increase sexual activity.

The implications of these findings about the pineal are truly astonishing. Here is a major component of human activity and sexuality that until recently was completely unsuspected and un-documented—a hidden response to sensory input that is only now being discovered. How many other sensory systems are there, then, that play just as significant a role but which have not come along in scientific research even as far as the pineal?

One of these, already mentioned in Chapter 7, may be the vomeronasal system, the parallel olfactory sense which in nonhumans is responsible for detecting chemical signals given off by members of the same species. A component of perspiration given off in times of anxiety and fear, for instance, may originally have served to warn those around us of possible dangers, as it does in many other species. Other chemicals emitted by the body seem to have just the opposite effect, attracting potential sexual partners to us at times when we are most likely to copulate. What, then, of the possibility that there are as yet completely unmeasurable chemical signals to which we respond completely unknowingly?

Is it not also possible that some people are more sensitive to certain signals, giving them the equivalent of a different sensory system? There is a corollary in sense blindness. Nearly half of us, for example, are "odor blind" to the smell of urine. Over a third cannot smell malt. Six percent cannot smell fish. Is it not possible that some "psychics" are merely those who, with heightened vomeronasal or olfactory senses, can actually detect a person's psychic state from his odor? If this seems completely far-fetched, consider that scientists at the Monell Chemical Senses Center are rapidly closing in on a series of diagnostic tests which can accurately sense a person's physical condition by analyzing the total odor profile given off by the body. Perhaps psychics are already doing this.

There are constantly forces in the environment that we detect subliminally, which make their way into the brain or other organs and possibly affect behavior, but we are completely unaware of the presence of these forces and do not even understand what sensory organs, if any, might be involved. This is the case, for instance, with healing. The connection between the psyche and the soma (physical body) is obviously powerful, but in many cases the specific mechanisms are simply not known yet. A reputable study shows that the susceptibility to cancer within seven years after suffering a major object loss (a job, a close relative, a house, etc.) is far, far greater than normal. But what could be the mechanism? Some researchers have begun experimenting with "image treatments" for cancer, using a series of mental images to cure the cancer once it has been detected. As this book goes to press, scientists report that the natural endorphins mentioned previously in connection with pain have just been found to affect the immune system. What other as-yet-unknown forces in the environment, mediated by yet-unknown sensory processes, might be involved in the body's defensive responses against disease?

Plainly, healing and faith healing enter into the picture of extra-sensory perceptions in a very meaningful way. We have already noted the effect the healer may have in eliminating pain by stimulating the body's own production of endorphins. Acupuncture, too, is now a commonly accepted pain treatment at hospitals around the country. And what of other physical ailments? We keep coming back to the same observation: simply because science cannot yet explain or prove a link between two phenonema does not mean that they are not connected.

An example is the medicine man of the American Indian cultures who used a combination of pure illusion and pure belief to accomplish what in other religions are called miracles. Here is part of an account of the actions of a Dakota Indian medicine man, described by Natalie Curtis in *The Indians' Book:*

> On the banks of a thickly wooded creek the people camped, and there came to them a medicine man who said, "Give me of your bracelets and your rings, and in return I will do so much for you that you will feel no sickness for as long as my own life shall endure."
>
> They gave him bracelets and rings, both of buffalo-hide and of silver, and then the medicine man told them to make for him a sweat-lodge, such as the people call "new life," because the man that comes out of it feels as if made anew. So when he had purified himself in solitude, he set up a pole in the earth, and bound upon it a buffalo calf's hide painted red. Then the crier went throughout the camp and called for all the sick to come close to the pole, and when they were gathered there they cut off strips of skin from their arms for an offering and laid them at the foot of the pole. Then came forth the medicine man, and he set a wooden cup at the foot of the pole, and began to sing.
>
> While he sang, water trickled down the pole until it filled the cup. He gave the cup to the sick, and they all drank of the water and were healed, yet the cup was never empty.

The medicine man has apparently gained the faith of his audience to the point that he can perform magical feats which the audience will accept as reality. And with that faith, he performs the healing ceremony, making the audience believe that healing can be accomplished with the same ease as the other feats of magic.

Are the teachings of Christian Science any less valid? What power does the faith healer exert if not a combination of the powerful placebo effect with what may amount to a specific form of electromagnetic energy which actually heals in the same way that physical therapists use ultrasound devices and heat lamps?

This discussion of natural phenomena and how they are detected or responded to by the body is somehow satisfying to the rational mind, offering explanations for various observations that might otherwise remain "mysterious." But the rational explanations cannot help when it comes to the most fundamental extra-sensory experience: that very, very special feeling when a psychic phenomenon occurs. For example, thinking of a friend or relative not heard from in months when suddenly the phone rings and the person is on the line. Or when one gets a "flash" that something is about to happen or has just happened hundreds of miles away. Or when one suddenly *knows* exactly what is going to be said before it is uttered, or exactly what something will look like before it is seen. These are the psychic experiences for which science, in all its rational glory, cannot help with an answer.

In this sense, *extra-sensory* really does mean outside the range of normal sensory experiences, not simply an adjunct to them. It is not even clear that these extra-sensory experiences are truly sensory —that is, they may be completely internal, within the person who perceives them, and not manifestations of the real world at all. And certainly the sensory system that receives them, if one is involved, is shrouded in utmost mystery.

These ESP phenomena are probably the same as those experienced by people being tested for psi abilities with a special deck of cards on which are printed colors and symbols. Those who have natural psychic abilities predict, with greater accuracy than chance would allow, which card the tester is holding. Some people are better at it than others, suggesting that it really may be a sensory experience after all, which, like vision and hearing and tasting and touching, has different levels of acuity. But there is no doubt, once the mental image of the card flashes in the mind, that something truly "extra" is going on.

If psychic perception does occur through some sensory system that allows a person to literally snatch thoughts and images out of the air, what can be the means through which the images are received? The most likely explanation is that some kind of sensing of electromagnetic radiation is involved, but through a mechanism

which is still totally hidden. In this way, the electromagnetic vibratory frequencies of colors themselves could be perceived directly. And this could also correspond, of course, with the sources of electromagnetic energy emanating from the body. The kinds of brain signals detected by the SQUID are extremely weak, however, and would only account for the kind of psi experiences that occur at close range.

James Beal of NASA's Marshall Space Flight Center suggests, therefore, that microwave energy in the "X-band" (around 9 gigahertz) might be involved. This frequency, which falls within the bands used in commercial broadcast applications (when a news crew goes live, it sends back signals to the station on either 2, 7 or 13 GHz), is a frequency at which many living organisms seem to emit radiation. The suggestion is that life processes in the human body somehow modify the radiation, in a process analogous to how radio and television signals are created, and then "transmit" the modified radiation to others who can somehow receive the modified signal in a way analogous to the home television or radio set.

In this regard, it is worth mentioning some of the body's responses to other natural forces such as electricity, which may be involved in psychic phenomena; the responses are not necessarily based on a separate sensory system, but are nonetheless detected and acted upon. Static electricity, for example, is a major natural force which can affect the body directly, in the same way that microwaves are absorbed. Static makes the nerves of the brain and the rest of the nervous system fire more easily and generally makes a person more alert. Discrimination of levels of a light's brightness is increased in the presence of static as is the brain's ability to perceive the difference between a light flickering rapidly and a solid glow.

Similarly, there are the various phenomena associated with positively-charged electrical fields and the negative flow of free ions—the kinds of effects supposedly achieved by the "ion generators" people claim are so beneficial. Peacefulness, tranquility, improved healing—all are claimed as results of keeping a flow of negative ions in the air.

On the other hand, changes in the negative ion supply are met

with quite the reverse reaction—depression, lethargy, and so forth. This is the case when an approaching storm causes a build-up of positive ions in the air, perhaps slowing the flow of electricity in the nervous system.

Without a specific sensory system to detect them, these various forms of energy are simply forces to which the body responds—as it reacts, for example, to taking aspirin even though there is no "aspirin sensing" system. But the possibility that there is an as-yet-unknown sensory mechanism at work cannot be ruled out. For considering that the entire nervous system depends on the passage of minute electrical spikes along the nerve pathways, it would not be surprising at all to find that the transmission was either aided or hindered by large amounts of electricity present in the environment.

One other phenomenon of electricity is worth mentioning here. In literature as in real life it has been noted frequently that animals seem to know beforehand when danger such as an earthquake is brewing—barking or crying out, trying to break free, and so forth. The thought has been that animals are somehow psychic, that they simply "know" that danger is coming, just as dogs are sometimes reported to know that something has happened to their master even though a great physical distance separates them.

We have no explanation for most of these phenomena, but animals' ability to predict earthquakes can be attributed to a phenomenon of static electricity, according to observations made by Helmut Tributsch of the Free University of Berlin while researching in the Peruvian Andes. Human skin is quite damp, due to secretions of the sweat glands and of the oil glands at the base of the hair follicles. By contrast, most animals have relatively dry skin. And when the electromagnetic disturbances that are now known to precede an earthquake occur, large amounts of static electricity build up in the air. This causes the animal's fur to become quite "electrified," literally bristling with the static charge, an effect that is intensified when the animal is in an enclosed space, such as a house or a barn. So the animal that seems to sense the coming of disaster is merely extremely uncomfortable. No wonder horses try to break free, dogs bark violently, and cats move their kittens out of doors.

Another suggestion is that the communication might happen on a much lower frequency. The earth itself is constantly vibrating, anywhere between .1 and 100 times a second, with an average frequency just around 10 hertz. In this same frequency, falling in a range between 8 and 13 hertz, is the brain wave pattern associated with REM sleep and dreaming. This is also the frequency of light flashes or rapid-fire sounds that can bring on an epileptic seizure. The possibility, according to scientists working in this field, is that minute changes in this natural vibratory frequency might account for profound psychic changes and perceptions.

Yet despite all these possible explanations, true psi experiences really do lie outside our current ability to account for them. Some will probably prove to be sensory experiences after all, information perceived about the environment through a sense organ such as the pineal gland or the vomeronasal organ. These senses were discovered through increasingly sophisticated surgical techniques on animals, an area of science that is still under development. There are also parts of the brain which are known today whose functions are not yet completely clear. If one of these is involved in sensing an additional part of the electromagnetic spectrum, however, then the groundwork for establishing a link between the body's hormone/enzyme processes and some as-yet-unknown environmental factor can be clearly established. As it stands now, however, about the only thing that is known about the science of psi phenomena is that they seem to be matched fairly closely with alpha waves—electrical signals produced by the brain when it is engaged in activities such as dreaming and creative thought.

This somewhat inconclusive ending is not, perhaps, what might be expected of a discussion which has revealed some truly astonishing scientific discoveries about the sensory systems and how they work. It is in the nature of scientific inquiry and scientific thought to expect that all things should be understandable in the rational cosmos that science portrays. But the unanswered questions, the next frontier that science must push back, are unfortunately also part of the picture. We are probably closer today to deciphering the mysteries of the sensory systems than we have ever been in the past;

and yet the "ultimate answer" is always a stone's throw away, no matter how close we get.

Science has its place in the modern world. But magic and mystery have their place, too, particularly when it comes to research on the senses. And as soon as one mystery is brought to light by the efforts of science, so another one becomes evident in the essential darkness of the inner mind.

The mysteries about the body, and specifically the sensory systems, are essentially like features inside a huge, dark cave. Science has come in with larger and larger flashlights, illuminating more and more of the features, showing how one connects with the other. But the cave is mammoth, and no flashlight will probably ever fully penetrate its depths.

Bibliography

CHAPTER 1: THE SEVENTEEN SENSES

Barlow, H., and Mollon, J. 1982. *The Senses.* Cambridge, Engl.:
Cambridge University Press.

Bartoshuk, L. 1980. Separate worlds of taste. *Psychology Today,*
September, pp. 48–63.

Gouras, P. 1981. "Visual System IV: Color Vision." In *Principles of
Neural Science,* E. Kandel and J. Schwartz, eds. New York: Elsevier
North-Holland, Inc.

Hitchcock, C. 1983. Machine vision—A systems approach. *Electronic
Imaging,* 2(1), 32–35.

Hubel, D., and Wiesel, T. 1979. Brain mechanisms of vision. *Scientific
American,* 241(9), 150–163.

Hudspeth, A. 1983. The hair cells of the inner ear. *Scientific American,*
248(1), 54–64.

Kinnucan, P. 1981. How smart robots are becoming smarter. *High
Technology,* 1(1), 32–40.

Leukel, F. 1972. *Introduction to Physiological Psychology,* 2nd ed. St. Louis,
Mo.: The C. V. Mosby Co.

Ziegler, H. P. 1975. The sensual feel of food. *Psychology Today,* August,
pp. 62–66.

CHAPTER 2: PAIN

Blau, M. 1982. Conquering pain. *New York Magazine,* March 22, pp. 26–31.

Bonica, J. 1979. *Advances in Pain Research and Therapy,* Vol. 3. New York: Raven Press.

Bonica, J., and Albe-Fessard, A. 1976. *Advances in Pain Research and Therapy,* Vol. 1. New York: Raven Press.

Eccles, J. 1973. *The Understanding of the Brain.* New York: McGraw-Hill.

Hilgard, E., and Hilgard, J. 1975. *Hypnosis in the Relief of Pain.* Los Altos, Calif.: William Kaufmann Inc.

Lowenstein, O. 1966. *The Senses.* Baltimore: Penguin Books.

Ng, L., and Bonica, J. 1980. *Pain, Discomfort and Humanitarian Care.* New York: Elsevier North-Holland, Inc.

Uttal, W. 1973. *The Psychobiology of Sensory Coding.* New York: Harper & Row.

Van Dyke, C., and Byck, R. 1982. Cocaine. *Scientific American, 246*(3), 128–141.

Wurtman, R. 1982. Nutrients that modify brain function. *Scientific American, 246*(4), 50–59.

CHAPTER 3: TWO DIFFERENT WORLDS . . .

Binkley, S. 1979. A timekeeping enzyme in the pineal gland. *Scientific American, 240,* 66–71.

Bissinger, B. 1983. The role of the parietal eye in the homing behavior of the lizard, *Sceloporus jarrovi.* Doctoral dissertation, City University of New York.

Blackmore, R., and Frankel, R. 1981. Magnetic navigation in bacteria. *Scientific American, 245*(6), 58–65.

Brown, J. 1975. *The Evolution of Behavior.* New York: W. W. Norton.

Grinnel, A., and Hagiwara, S. 1972. Adaptations of the auditory system for echolocation. *Z. vergl. Physiologie, 76,* 41–81.

Kalmijn, A. 1982. Electric and magnetic field detection in elasmobranch fishes. *Science, 218,* 916–918.

Knudsen, E. 1981. The hearing of the barn owl. *Scientific American,* 245(12), 112–125.

Levine, J., and MacNichol, E. 1982. Color vision in fishes. *Scientific American,* 246(2), 140–149.

Michener, C. 1974. *The Social Behavior of the Bees: A Comparative Study.* Cambridge, Mass.: Harvard University Press.

Moller, P. 1980. Electroperception. *Oceanus, 23,* 44–54.

Newman, E., and Hartline, P. 1982. The infrared "vision" of snakes. *Scientific American,* 246(3), 116–127.

Porter, K. 1972. *Herpetology.* Philadelphia: W. B. Saunders Co.

Regal, P. 1978. "Behavioral Differences Between Reptiles and Mammals: An Analysis of Activity and Mental Capabilities." In *Behavior and Neurology of Lizards: An Interdisciplinary Colloquium,* N. Greenberg and P. MacLean, eds., Rockville, Md.: National Institute of Mental Health.

Webster, D. 1965. Ears of Dipodomys: Adaptations allow kangaroo rat to meet stresses of desert life. *Natural History, 74,* 26–33.

Weiner, J. 1982. Tree Talk. *The Sciences, 22*(8), 5.

CHAPTER 4: TABULA RASA: THE DEVELOPMENT OF THE HUMAN SENSORY SYSTEMS

Annis, L. 1978. *The Child Before Birth.* Ithaca, N.Y.: Cornell University Press.

Armitage, S., Baldwin, B., and Vince, M. 1980. The fetal sound environment of sheep. *Science, 208,* 1235–1236.

Barlow, H., and Mollon, J. 1982. *The Senses.* Cambridge, Engl.: Cambridge University Press.

Bower, T. 1982. *Development in Infancy,* 2nd ed. San Francisco: W. H. Freeman and Co.

Constantine-Paton, M., and Law, M. 1982. The development of maps and stripes in the brain. *Scientific American,* 247(12), 62–70.

Davidson, R., and Fox, N. 1982. Asymmetrical brain activity discriminates between positive and negative affective stimuli in human infants. *Science, 218,* 1235–1236.

Field, R., Woodson, R., Greenberg, R., and Cohen, D. 1982. Discrimination and imitation of facial expressions by neonates. *Science, 218,* 179–181.

Fox, R., and McDaniel, C. 1982. The perception of biological motion by human infants. *Science, 218,* 486–487.

Jones-Molfese, V. 1977. Responses of neonates to colored stimuli. *Child Development, 48,* 1092–1095.

Klineberg, O. 1954. *Social Psychology,* rev. ed. New York: Holt.

Piaget, J. 1970. *Main Trends in Interdisciplinary Research.* New York: Harper & Row.

Pines, M. 1981. The civilizing of Genie. *Psychology Today,* September, pp. 28–34.

CHAPTER 5: THE HUMAN SEMAPHORE: THE LANGUAGES OF NONVERBAL SENSORY COMMUNICATION

Alford, R., and Alford, K. F. 1981. Sex differences in asymmetry in the facial expression of emotion. *Neuropsychologia, 19*(4), 605–608.

Busniakova, M. 1977. Preference of colours and coloured stimulus structures depending on age. *Psychologia a Patopsychologia Dielala, 12,* 401–410.

Cimbalo, R., Beck, K., and Sendziak, D. 1978. Emotionally toned pictures and color selection for children and college students. *Journal of Genetic Psychology, 133*(2), 303–304.

Darakis, L. 1977. Influence of five stimulus colors on GSR. *Bulletin de Psychologie, 30*(14–16), 760–766.

Farne, M., and Campione, F. 1976. Colour as an indicator for distance: Colour per se or contrast with the background? *Giornale Italiano di Psicologia, 3*(3), 415–420.

Goldberg, F. 1977. Affective associations by Japanese pre-school children to black and white boxes. *Psychological Reports, 40*(2), 515–521.

Heller, W., and Levy, J. 1981. Perception and expression of emotion in right-handers and left-handers. *Neuropsychologia, 19*(2), 263–272.

Hess, E. 1975. The role of pupil size in communication. *Scientific American, 233*(5), 110–119.

Knowles, P. 1977. The "blue seven" is not a phenomenon. *Perceptual and Motor Skills, 45*(2), 648–650.

Reuter-Lorenz, P., and Davidson, R. 1981. Differential contributions of the two cerebral hemispheres to the perception of happy and sad faces. *Neuropsychologia, 19*(4), 609–613.

Sackeim, H., Gur, R., and Saucy, M. 1978. Emotions are expressed more intensely on the left side of the face. *Science, 202,* 434-435.

Schickinger, P. 1975. Intercultural comparisons of the emotional connotations of colors in the Chromatic Pyramid projective test, using factor analysis. *Revista de Psicologia General y Applicada, 30* (136), 781–808.

CHAPTER 7: MAKING SCENTS

Brown, J. 1975. *The Evolution of Behavior.* New York: W. W. Norton.

Henkin, R. 1982. "Olfaction in Human Disease." In *Otolaryngology,* G. English, ed. Philadelphia: Harper & Row Publishers Inc.

Kubie, J., Vagvolgyi, A., and Halpern, M. 1978. Roles of the vomeronasal and olfactory systems in courtship behavior of male garter snakes. *Journal of Comparative and Physiological Psychology, 92,* 627–641.

Labows, J. 1980. What the nose knows: Investigating the significance of human odors. *The Sciences,* November, pp. 11–13.

Maugh, T. 1982. The scent makes sense. *Science, 215,* 1224.

Meredith, M., and Burghardt, G. 1978. Electrophysiological studies of the tongue and accessory olfactory bulb in garter snakes. *Physiology and Behavior, 21,* 1001–1008.

Michael, R., Keverne, E., and Bonsall, R. 1971. Pheromones: Isolation of male sex attractants from a female primate. *Science, 172,* 964–966.

Powers, J., and Winans, S. 1975. Vomeronasal organ: Critical role in mediating sexual behavior of the male hamster. *Science, 187,* 961–963.

Simon, C. 1982. Masters of the tongue flick. *Natural History, 91,* 58–67.

White, D. 1981. Pursuit of the ultimate aphrodisiac. *Psychology Today,* September, pp. 9–12.

Wysocki, C. 1978. Neurobehavioral evidence for the involvement of the vomeronasal system in mammalian reproduction. *Neuroscience and Biobehavioral Reviews, 3,* 301–341.

Wysocki, C., Wellington, J., and Beauchamp, G. 1980. Access of urinary nonvolatiles to the mammalian vomeronasal organ. *Science, 207,* 781–783.

CHAPTER 8: ILLUSION AND REALITY

Attneave, F. 1971. Multistability in perception. *Scientific American,*
    225(6), 63–71.
Castaneda, C. 1968. *The Teachings of Don Juan: A Yaqui Way of*
    Knowledge. Berkeley: University of California Press, pp. 46–
    47.
DeGivry, G. 1971. *Witchcraft, Magic and Alchemy.* New York: Dover
    Publications.
Dixon, N. 1971. *Subliminal Perception: The Nature of a Controversy.*
    London: McGraw-Hill.
Eliade, M. 1972. *Shamanism: Archaic Techniques of Ecstasy.* Princeton,
    N.J.: Princeton University Press, pp. 230–231.
Haber, R. 1980. Eidetic images are not just imaginary. *Psychology Today,*
    November, pp. 72–82.
Jung, C. G. 1933. *Modern Man in Search of a Soul.* New York: Harcourt
    Brace.
Kelly, D. 1981. "Physiology of Sleep and Dreaming." In *Principles of*
    Neural Science, E. Kandel and J. Schwartz, eds. New York: Elsevier
    North-Holland, Inc.
Kelly, D. 1981. "Disorders of Sleep and Consciousness." In *Principles of*
    Neural Science, E. Kandel and J. Schwartz, eds. New York: Elsevier
    North-Holland, Inc.
Key, W. 1973. *Subliminal Seduction.* Englewood Cliffs, N.J.: New
    American Library.
Marks, L. 1975. Synesthesia: The lucky people with mixed-up senses.
    Psychology Today, June, pp. 48–52.
Nassau, K. 1980. The causes of color. *Scientific American, 243,* 124–
    155.
Packard, V. 1957. *The Hidden Persuaders.* New York: David McKay Co.
Rock, I. 1974. The perception of disoriented figures. *Scientific American,*
    230, 78–85.
Siegel, R. 1977. Hallucinations. *Scientific American, 237,* 132–140.
Siegel, R., and West, L. 1975. *Hallucinations: Behavior, Experience, and*
    Theory. New York: John Wiley and Sons.
Teuber, M. 1974. Sources of ambiguity in the prints of Maurits C.
    Escher. *Scientific American, 231*(1), 90–104.

CHAPTER 9: EXTRA-SENSORY PERCEPTION

Baker, R. 1981. *Human Navigation and the Sixth Sense*. New York: Simon and Schuster.

Beal, J. 1974. "The Emergence of Paraphysics: Research and Applications." In *Psychic Exploration: A Challenge for Science*, E. Mitchell. New York: G. P. Putnam's Sons.

Brenner, D., Williamson, S., and Kaufman, L. 1975. Visually evoked magnetic fields of the human brain. *Science, 190*, pp. 480–482.

Crookall, R. 1964. *More Astral Projections: Analyses of Case Histories*. London: Aquarian, pp. 72–75.

Curtis, Natalie. 1950. *The Indians' Book*. New York: Dover Publications, pp. 52.

Dean, E. 1974. "Precognition and Retrocognition." In *Psychic Exploration: A Challenge for Science*, E. Mitchell. New York: G. P. Putnam's Sons.

Fishman, J., and Allen, W. H. 1964. *My Darling Clementine*. London: Pan.

Gevins, A., Doyle, J., Cutillo, B., Schaffer, R., Tannehill, R., Ghannam, J., Gilcrease, V., and Yeager, C. 1981. Electrical potentials in human brain during cognition: New method reveals dynamic patterns of correlation. *Science, 213*, pp. 918–921.

Jung, C. G. 1933. *Modern Man in Search of a Soul*. New York: Harcourt Brace.

Kaufman, L., and Williamson, S. 1980. The evoked magnetic field of the human brain. *Annals of the New York Academy of Sciences, 340*, pp. 45–65.

Morris, R. 1974. "The Psychobiology of Psi." In *Psychic Exploration: A Challenge for Science*, E. Mitchell. New York: G. P. Putnam's Sons.

Rhine, L. E. 1954. Frequency of types of experience in spontaneous precognition. *Journal of Parapsychology, 18*.

Tart, C. 1974. "Out-of-the-Body Experiences." In *Psychic Exploration: A Challenge for Science*, E. Mitchell. New York: G. P. Putnam's Sons.

Tributsch, H. 1982. A seismic sense. *The Sciences, 22*(9), pp. 24–28.

Williamson, S., Kaufman, L., and Brenner, D. 1978. Latency of the neuromagnetic response of the human visual cortex. *Vision Research, 18*(1), pp. 107–110.

Wolfe, William Thomas. 1978. *And the Sun is Up: Kundalini Rises in the West*. Milan, New York: Academy Hill Press.

Zoeger, J., Dunn, J., and Fuller, M. 1981. Magnetic material in the head of the common Pacific dolphin. *Science, 213,* pp. 892–894.

Index